My RADIUS

~ *The Story of RADIUS Church* ~

J.T. Reeves

First Edition
(Summer, 2020)

This Book is dedicated to the RADIUS family from years past and present. I could include only a handful of your names in these few pages, but you know who you are and how much you mean to us.

Thank you...

Table of Contents

Author, Audience, and Breakdown

Being the son of a church planter can probably be most accurately compared with a rollercoaster ride. I moved nine times in my first eighteen years of life. I've lived in five different states, attended seven different grade schools, and been a part of six different church plants.

I use "been a part of" very lightly because my contribution to the church in my younger years consisted of drinking the leftover grape juice and eating the remaining bread from communion—and then maybe wrestling with a couple chairs that were twice my size for set-up or tear-down.

But I *felt* like a big part of our church plants—and statistically I was. Dad always jokes that at the beginning of Radius Church there were only twelve members, and half of the church (including me) were his kids. I think I took a lot of pride in that knowledge, that I was an important member of the church, that I knew everyone, and that they knew me, and that I was fortunate enough to be there to witness the beginning...

Now, I have the privilege of reflecting on those years where I thought I knew everything and everyone. I was given the task of writing the history of Radius Church in narrative form, and through various personal interviews, much research, and many, *many* stories, I have finally compiled this summation of Radius's history.

The book is comprised of six **Stages**, which were delineated by the Radius Elders, and which are divided further into **Parts**. The Parts are then split into a plethora of

Stories that come directly from the interviewees. Anything in "quotations" is a direct quote from an interview.

This book is not perfect. Many of the things I've written may not be perfect representations. People might have remembered details incorrectly. I might have misunderstood or misportrayed nuances in the stories.

But our hope is not in our ability to write perfect stories; our hope is in a perfect Savior, and that through our imperfect stories others in our radius would long to know Him more fully.

Ultimately, the purpose of this book is to record the history of this beautiful, though messy, work that God did to bring Radius Church into existence. We never want to forget what He has done, and we always want to look forward to what He can do with a handful of men and women who are obedient to His call.

What do you want people to see out of this book or to know about Radius?

(in the words of the Radius leaders)

"I want people to understand Radius's generosity—radical generosity that guided our decisions."

"I want people to know just how special it is. When you really serve a group of people, they become closer than family. And people should see the sacrifice... This thing is an investment."

"The church is not a building. Know your neighbor's name. Prayer, prayer, *prayer*. Those were the things we stood for."

"There is nothing that *we* did that has made Radius successful. The only reason we have people in the seats is because of God. This is really a story about God's favor on a bunch of knuckleheads."

"How important solid community is. Radius is like family to me... And the extravagant generosity—it really isn't something we just said. It's something we *did*."

"The faithfulness of God in the midst of our tom-foolery. The highlight is God's work. There's no one here that has the ability to make that kind of impression on a community."

"Radius church exists to glorify God by making disciples, planting churches, and living generously."

Stage 1

Birth (2003-2004)

Part 1: "Before the beginning"

Technically, Radius Church began in 2003. That's when the
name "Radius" came about. That's when Radius Church
started holding services. That's what most people like to call
"the beginning." But, as I've been told so many times, the
Church is not a building, or a service, or a time—it's the
people. And the people came together well before 2003...

DCF (Downtown Community Fellowship)

In 1995, John and Cheryl Reeves took up all they had
and moved from Dubuque, Iowa to Clemson, South
Carolina. They didn't have a house. Didn't have a job. Just
three children and an '81 rickety maroon Chevy Nova.

Why? Well, to give you the shortest version possible:
John and Cheryl felt called by God to go out and be church
planters. The tough part? Neither of them really knew what
"church planting" actually meant. All the same, they firmly
believed it was what God was prodding them to do, and
they wanted to be obedient to God—which meant giving up
John's job, packing up the house, and moving their family
nine hundred miles to be near the Clemson University
campus.

Over the next few years, the young couple (both in their late twenties) found favor with God, and He blessed their mission. During that time, John and Cheryl Reeves, Matt and Jenny Reeves, and James and Rachel Frazee generously poured out their time, resources, and energy to the Clemson community (*remember those names*).

John and Cheryl soon developed an "open-door policy" with the young twenty-somethings in the area. College students, singles, and young couples would literally walk in the door at any moment of the day to talk, eat, or simply because, well, they *lived* with the Reeves.

I know what you're thinking. There's no possible way Cheryl allowed multiple college guys to live in her basement while she was pregnant with her fourth child. While she had infants, babies, and elementary kids to take care of. And while John had to start his own landscaping business (brilliantly named "Yard Dawg") to support their family.

Talk about crazy.

Jeremiah Jones, Salim Khalil, and Duncan Pleming were just a few of many young men who made their home in the Reeves' basement (*these names are important too*). Soon, Trisha Watson (soon-to-be Trisha *Kirkland*), Brian Kirkland (who happened to be chasing Trisha), Amanda Shepherd (soon-to-be Amanda *Khalil*) and many others were starting to come and sit on the Reeves' back deck to pray, teach, fellowship, and worship God.

And the seeds of a church plant suddenly began to grow.

After hopping from location to location, the *extremely* young leaders of what would be called Downtown

Community Fellowship (DCF) discovered a print shop near Clemson's Little John Coliseum. Without funds, they agreed to rent the building—praying God would provide the means for them to meet and grow there.

That's when they realized that Clemson football was back in action (go tigers). And the print shop was in an excellent location near the stadium. Parking spots for Clemson games were limited...

For $5, then $10, then $20 a spot, the DCF church found a way to pay for their building via parking cars. After painting hundreds of rusty chairs purchased cheap from a bingo joint and acquiring a giant fan they would set in the back of the room each week (the AC didn't work), the place was ready for use on Sundays.

That's how this church began. DCF was the first church plant. Then DCF Athens (now One Hope Church). Then North Perimeter. Then Lifehouse (now Graystone Community Church). Then Oasis and Radius.

....

The DCF Church created a deep bond between many of the future leaders of Radius. Pastors, worship leaders, technical workers, children's ministry leaders, elders, and prayer warriors worked together for several years before many of these young believers went their separate ways. The Reeves moved to Georgia—and Brian and Trisha Kirkland followed close behind before moving to Wheaton, Illinois. Jeremiah Jones too would go on to serve at North Perimeter Church in Georgia before ending up in Florida. Duncan Pleming moved to Northeast Columbia. And Salim and Amanda Khalil made their way to Lexington, South Carolina.

Lexington: a town Cheryl Reeves had never heard of until the year 2003. As you might have guessed, she was about to become very, *very* familiar with it.

"I had never heard of Lexington before"

"Restless." That's how Cheryl Reeves felt in the Spring of 2003. And maybe that sensation just made sense. After all, she had six kids (all elementary-age or younger) and happened to be in the thick of planting another church, *Lifehouse*.

Cheryl was also working to make her house in Snellville, Georgia feel like a real *home*. They had lived there for three years now, and she was beginning to hope that this location—unlike the previous five before—would actually become a place where she could put down some roots.

Still, she felt restless.

That Spring, John decided to visit Lexington, South Carolina to meet with Jeff Shipman, a fellow church planter who was involved with Crossroads Church in Columbia. John did things like this on a regular basis, and Cheryl had no reason to suspect this occasion would prove to be anything more than what it was supposed to be: a meeting.

But when Cheryl saw him that night, she immediately sensed something in his demeanor. Something she had seen several times before.

Cheryl suggested they put their six kids to bed early, and after the last goodnight, she demanded he spill whatever was on his mind.

"I think we're supposed to move there," he said.

That's when Cheryl started sobbing. Not because she was going to be dragged against her will to some place she had never heard of. But because she was going by God's Will, and she knew in her heart, by what she called a "supernatural feeling," that His Will was for their family to move to Lexington. Her *restlessness* could now be put at ease.

Less than 24 hours later, I climbed into our plum purple minivan, crammed in my reserved middle-left car-seat, and we headed toward Lexington to check out the town in which we would live for the next three years. When we returned, we began packing, cleaning, and staging (mostly I just watched), anticipating the daunting task of selling our house.

Two years earlier, John (my dad) and Cheryl (my mom) had placed the house on the market in order to move closer to their church plant. After several months, no one offered to buy it, and they removed it from the market, taking it as a sign from the Lord to stay.

This time, the house sold within days.

They took it as a sign from the Lord to go.

SIDE-NOTE: As John Reeves was walking and praying outside in Columbia, a college student drove by with windows down, making an obscene gesture and shouting "F*** YOU!" as he drove past. John Reeves told me it was right then that he knew Lexington was where he wanted to be.

....

In late April of 2003 Salim Khalil received word that the Reeves were thinking of moving to Lexington. At the time, the Khalil's were visiting churches around Lexington, searching for a place where they might plug in and become effective for the Lord in their town. So when Salim Khalil picked up the phone that summer and heard that the Reeves were, in fact, moving to Lexington to plant another church, they made what they called "a really easy decision." They felt this was exactly what they wanted to do.

Thus, the recruiting process began for John Reeves and the prayer process began for several single guys and families he contacted. John quickly contacted Jeremiah Jones (who had led worship at DCF in Clemson and North Perimeter in Georgia), telling Jeremiah he had a deep "since" that the Lord was calling Jeremiah to plant in Lexington with him (yes, he spelled it "since" and not "sense" in his email). The Lord must have been working, because despite John's spelling, Jeremiah was all in; he and John always had unique chemistry, and Jeremiah was ready for another adventure. Similarly, Duncan Pleming took little convincing as he began commuting from Northeast Columbia. But as excited as some of the young believers were, other families—good friends from DCF—felt called elsewhere and were not able to come. This proved to be a tough hit for the young church planters who were "crushed" with disappointment and a little shocked at how few had decided to join them.

But there you have it. In the summer of 2003 twelve individuals met in a small apartment in Lexington, South Carolina.

Eight of these twelve individuals had the last name *Reeves*.

Salim and Amanda Khalil, Duncan Pleming, Jeremiah Jones, and John and Cheryl Reeves—along with Zay, Moriah, Real, Chunk, one-year-old Malachi, and three-year-old me—would sit in that apartment and pray, and plan, and dream of what God might do for the Lexington community through their obedience to Him.

Six adults began meeting regularly and proclaiming the name of God together through prayer in their homes, seeking to plant a church in Lexington or Columbia, South Carolina.

....

A couple weeks. That's how long it took for the six adults to receive a building.

Yes, *receive*. A word synonymous with *"free gift."*

Rick Parks was Lead Pastor at Lexington Community Church off Park Road in Lexington. Lexington Community Church (LCC) had disbanded its elders and was contemplating shutting its doors, struggling to stay afloat. Trusting Jeff Shipman's recommendation of John's church planting and leadership skills, Rick Parks took a significant leap of faith and offered up the LCC building *and* its members. The building was a *free gift* from the leaders of LCC, and Rick, a former church planter himself, planted a seed with his own ministry in giving to Radius.

It was just the first of many crazy stories of God's kindness to this little group.

Even with this sudden opportunity, the young church planters still felt their hearts drawn to the downtown

Columbia area near the University of South Carolina. They began pursuing a place to meet in this vicinity. Soon enough, they found one...

Two churches, quite distinct and separate, emerged from the *same* small band of believers who worked to glorify the Lord in two different environments. In Lexington, **Oasis Church** began meeting in the old LCC building. In downtown Columbia, **Radius Church** began meeting in a coffee shop.

The Reeves moved. Salim and Amanda Khalil's lives drastically changed. Jeremiah Jones moved. Duncan Pleming's schedule filled and his gas tank emptied. And a group of other families would later follow suit, beginning to devote hours upon hours to this thing that we call the Church.

These people did (and still do) hard things because they believed (and still believe) that the end goal of life is not their personal happiness, but the glory of God.

Not that church planting wasn't fun. Trust me, little me got to experience a whole lot of crazy cool things.

Part 2: "The Church is not a building"

Downtown Columbia. Right outside the University of South Carolina. After dark. Downstairs in a basement...

No, this is not the location of a party. On the contrary, this is where Radius Church originated. This is the site where half of Radius' DNA was formed.

....

Jeremiah Jones walked into Jammin' Java, a coffee shop off Main Street in downtown Columbia, just a few blocks from the South Carolina Capital Building. It would not have been the average person's first choice of church building, but for Jeremiah and the other young leaders of this church, it was perfect.

Steps descended down the side of the main building to reveal the basement where Sunday night services would take place. Lights hung from the low ceiling. Huge poles stood in the center of the room. Bistro tables functioned as pews. And kids care was nonexistent.

Not long ago, Jeremiah listened in on a sermon of Jeff Shipman's at Crossroads Church. Shipman emphasized the idea that followers of Christ should be influencing every person within a ten-mile *radius*. That believers would actively serve their communities so their love for Jesus Christ would overflow onto their neighbors.

That's when the little group of believers who met in Jammin' Java were first named *Radius Church*. And in no time, the little church was in full swing.

Jeremiah's worship was a huge part of Radius's identity as a church, and he grew accustomed to popping strings from playing song after song after song following John's very unpredictable messages.

SIDE-NOTE: John would spend an hour—*ONE* hour—at McAlister's Deli planning his sermon. Yeesh. Then his message would generally include a challenge or call to worship that was new, spontaneous, and very unorthodox. Because of this, Jeremiah was basically on-call to lead worship (including *unplanned* worship) at any moment during the service.

Both out of sheer curiosity ("who would put a church in a basement coffee shop?"), and extensive inviting, college kids from the University of South Carolina and some young professionals began entering the scene. "It wasn't glamorous. It wasn't the stuff you dream about. Radius didn't explode overnight." And yet Radius was picking up momentum and the Lord was working and moving among their little downtown church body.

To Jeremiah, that made his weekly planning meetings, weekly rehearsals, graphic-making, songwriting, guitar practice, audio/tech work, set-up, tear down, bulletin-making, band recruiting and training, communications work, and Sunday singing worth it. Was it a lot? Certainly. Did he have little to no income from this? Absolutely.

But the leaders at Radius were making "an investment" in their community. And with the vast amounts of time and work it took to establish Radius, there came a vast amount of beautiful fulfillment and excitement in doing His work.

Soon, a large group of students in their early twenties (including a key group of single women) started forming a tightly knit bond as they set-up and tore-down on Sundays, and put on event after event after event in their community. For some of them, this was the first time they had learned to enjoy friendship and fun "outside the college party scene." They would meet in small groups during the week for bible studies, after church for ice cream and extra socializing, and pretty much any other time they could make a good excuse to hang out. They were beginning to see that they "were not alone" in their walk with Jesus—and that others were there to walk right alongside them.

SIDE-NOTE: these women (Becca Jones, Kim Lyle, Sarah Ashlin Pleming, Heather Jones, Gina Hancock, Chris Beres, Debbie Jowers, Alexa Stillwell, Heidi Bozard, Anne Patton, Emily Hannen, Alexis Langley, Laura Ferrell) became such good friends at Radius that now, more than fifteen years later, many of them still talk daily. Their initiative and passion helped spark the beginnings of Radius.

Imagine that. A core group of Clemson grads (Jeremiah Jones, Salim Khalil, Brian Kirkland, Duncan Pleming, etc.) joining forces with a bunch of Carolina students. Cool things were happening at Radius Church, and that was only the half of it...

Oasis Church (Lexington)

Thirty minutes away, Oasis Church in Lexington was meeting on Sunday mornings at the Lexington Community Church facility. John and the others were actively recruiting, meeting with other leaders, old friends, and new connections in the area. Soon, a few key couples began filling some of those navy blue chairs at Oasis, and the makings of a core team emerged.

Lin and Laurie Keesey were one of these couples. Though hardly in their forties, the Keesey's were the oldest couple at Oasis; hence, they were quickly labeled the "wise old people," or "the patron and matron of the church," and became much needed mentors within the church. Their story fit the description of several other families who began serving at Oasis in the ensuing months. The Keesey's were referred to Oasis while searching for a church and immediately became intrigued with this idea of "knowing the people in your radius" and "giving things away" for God's Kingdom. And after Lin went on a men's retreat with some of the Oasis guys, he was certain this was where they were supposed to be. Naturally, they jumped right in.

Another couple, Chris and Cortney Seeby, joined the core group of Oasis Church several months later. Ever since moving from DCF in Clemson, they had longed for another opportunity to be among believers who were "open" with their faith, and they found themselves quick to become deeply involved with the church. Little did they know they would only increase in their involvement and leadership for the next fifteen years.

Oasis Church bonded rapidly. They fasted one day each week for months, praying for God's leading and favor as they sought to make His name known through their area. Starting their fast after dinner on Wednesday, they would gather to break their fast with a meal and prayer on Thursday evening.

Meanwhile, they were *all* serving.

Literally, almost everyone at Oasis was serving together and individually. One of the early leaders told me this: "in my whole life I could remember maybe three times someone responded to a sermon. Folks did not express their faith. Faith was private." At Oasis, there was an expectation (often firmly communicated by John) to discuss, apply, and respond to worship or a sermon. There was an expectation to serve. And sometimes "[John's] intensity" when explaining those expectations was overwhelming for new visitors. But for those who elected to endure the persistent challenges from John, they were completely bought in.

It was all or nothing.

So the church in Lexington (Oasis) grew, and the church in Columbia (Radius) also grew. All the while the core group continued to meet and put in hours upon hours of prayer, service, and fellowship, building an exceptional camaraderie that proved to strengthen the church.

Speaking of building, Oasis was beginning to have an issue with theirs—and it provided an entirely new obstacle for John and the others.

Open-handed: Selling the building

Open-handed, open-handed, open-handed. Six different individuals described Radius' dealings with finances using that one phrase. The people at this church never want to cling to their *stuff*. They just don't hold their possessions, their money, or even their homes and livelihoods with a tightened and closed fist. On the contrary, everything is so loose sometimes it feels like it might fall.

But a constant trust-fall with God is much surer than your own two feet.

Dad said that line was too poetic, but considering he can't even spell "sense," I figured it was safe to ignore his suggestion.

....

One of the best problems to have in church planting is too few seats or too little space. All the same, it's still that: a problem. Only a few months after John and Cheryl and the others had started Oasis, the newly given Lexington

Community Church building was beginning to show signs of lacking potential.

But not for the reason you might expect.

Oasis Church still had plenty of room. In fact, they hadn't even tried multiple services yet. However, John Reeves had a bigger vision for this church. Already he was thinking about what it would look like for Oasis Church and Radius Church to merge... they would certainly need more room for growth than the old Lexington Community Church building could provide.

So in February of 2004, the elders agreed to sell it.

$250,000. That's how much Radius got for a building they had met in for less than a year. To this young church, a quarter million dollars seemed almost too large a number to comprehend. It was more than enough money to find some other place where they could begin to meet.

But they didn't keep a penny of that money.

The leadership of Oasis felt it was the right thing to do to give all $250,000 to the previous leaders of Lexington Community Church. Rick Parks and the leaders of LCC decided to use this money to give $200,000 to missionaries around the world.

The remaining $50,000 they generously gave back to Oasis.

And suddenly Oasis Church was without a building.

This was the manifestation of one of Radius' biggest core values. In fact, when asked, "What are the main things you want people to know about this church," one leader promptly and avidly replied, "The Church is not a building. It's never been about a building. It's the people—the believers—that make up the church. And wherever the believers are, that's where the Church is."

So whether in basements, bars, movie theaters, public schools, restaurants, or even back decks, these men and women have made do with whatever they had. Not to prove a point, but to use their resources most fully for God's glory.

And to reach their radius.

Part 3: "Arranged Marriage #1"

Oasis had little money and no building. Radius was meeting in a basement. John Reeves, Jeremiah Jones, and many of the other leaders were waking up extremely early on Sundays and going to bed extremely late, setting up, tearing down, planning *multiple* messages, leading *multiple* worship sets. Something was going to have to give.

Hence (as Kim Lyle put it) the first "Arranged Marriage" of Radius Church began.

Prayer, Prayer, Prayer

Have you ever prayed with someone? Maybe that sounds like a silly question if you're a Christian. But really— have you ever *prayed* with someone? Have you ever begged the Lord to move in your town, your friends, your family, or yourself and asked someone to pray that with you? Or have you ever sat down with a friend to pray for *their* town, *their* friends, *their* family, *their* sins and struggles?

If you have, you can probably understand the significance of prayer in the birth stages of a church plant.

Not only is it essential to ask God—who is the *only* Provider—to guide, grow, strengthen, and foster our efforts, but prayer is also crucial for **unity**. How can two Christians *not* be unified when they are praying in the *same* place at the *same* time for the *same* things to the *same* God?

············

It was 5 o'clock on a Wednesday morning.

Lin Keesey was sitting outside Crossroads Church with leaders from *both* Oasis and Radius. It was still dark outside, and the air was chilly per usual. Fifteen other men were sitting with him, praying out loud to the God of the Universe—confident He was listening to every word they said.

Each Wednesday morning they had been praying as a group for two hours in the early morning, sharing their weaknesses while professing God's perfections. Led by John, they would "pray the truth about themselves," confessing their flaws and celebrating their strengths before each other and before God. After this, they would "pray the truth about God," acknowledging and praising the greatness of God by telling Him who He is.

Today, though, they were also praying specifically about how they would lead their church body. They had broken up into several groups and Lin was seated with a few leaders of *Radius*—the young, hip group of mainly college kids who met in some Columbia coffeeshop. He, on the other hand, was primarily involved with Oasis, and didn't usually attend those late-night services.

Even so, the leaders of both church plants prayed together as one.

Sixteen men. Two churches. One purpose for one God.

To Lin, this was the "battle in the trenches." The battle no one would see. These men were the backbone of *both* churches, and their foundation is what the bodies of Radius and Oasis would lean upon. Radius and Oasis were, in effect, growing roots *together* through these prayer times.

....

The importance of prayer in the early stages of Radius cannot be stressed enough. Every meeting was highlighted with prayer. Every day these families were asking the Lord what He wanted them to do for Him. They continued to fast once a week as a church, attempting to fashion their habits around Christ. Decisions were made because these men and women believed they were doing what God desired.

> SIDE-NOTE: One of the prayer challenges in the early stages was for everyone to write the name of a non-Christian friend on three dominoes and set them in places where they could remember to pray for them daily. The idea was that if one domino fell, this domino would cause another to fall, and that domino would cause yet another to fall in love with Jesus— exponential growth. Several people I interviewed explained stories of dominoes that fell months and years after they began earnestly praying. One of the dominoes fell nearly *eight* years later.

Lin Keesey probably hates that I wrote about him in here, but I thought it necessary to communicate that he was just one of a few normal followers of Jesus who was putting in the hours to see the changes he craved—changes he wanted not for himself but for God's glory. The unity in purpose and prayer provided stability to this group of believers as they rolled with the audibles that were being called to cope with the churches' growth.

And an "audible" (football term for "changed play-call," I'm assuming most of y'all know what this means) was exactly what they needed right now. As mentioned earlier, Oasis and Radius were both in interesting building predicaments, and the leaders of Radius were weary from the complications of two churches, two locations, and one leadership team.

So, in the summer of 2004 the core group of Radius and Oasis held a meeting to discuss the future of both churches. They all met at a house in downtown Columbia to pray, and to talk, and to argue, and to pray some more, and to discuss some more.

In the end, it was obvious that two churches with the same leaders was simply insufficient usage of manpower and resources. Lexington Community Church and Jammin' Java were both lacking space and potential. The churches should instead *combine* and meet in a new facility that would allow for growth. The tough part? The merged group would meet in *Lexington*.

For many of the Jammin' Java believers, this would be a tough blow. Most of them lived in Columbia, which meant it would be much more difficult to invite friends and connect their community to their church. Not to mention travel time.

But all in all, the decision was made, though they all agreed it was a "temporary" decision. **Radius Church** (this was the name of the new *combined* church) was to meet at Midway Elementary School for a short interval of time until they could find another building.

They had no idea they would be there for the next seven years.

In the summer of 2003, a small group of men and women came together in Lexington, S.C. and Columbia, S.C. to plant a church. That year, Radius Church and Oasis Church began as two separate bodies. But by the Fall of 2004, the two churches merged, planning to meet in Midway Elementary School.

Hustle (2004-2007)

Part 1: "Crazy Generous"

To say "generosity" was a theme during the interview process would be a colossal understatement. Every. Single. Interview. That's how many people mentioned Radius' generosity—I kid you not. Every single person I sat down and spoke with, whether by phone or in person, mentioned the "crazy," "extravagant," "incredible" generosity that could be seen in every part of the early Radius Church. I don't just mean $$ (although this was a part of it), but time. These young men and women were giving up the best parts of their days, their weeks, their lives to serve their community.

And they were doing some crazy things.

Movies in the Park/Newspapers/Mountain Dews/Roses
MOVIES: Laurie Keesey loved serving. Always had. So when Radius decided to offer movies at Finlay Park in Columbia to anyone who was willing to watch, she was all in.

Set up a screen, pop a little popcorn, buy some sodas, and maybe some people would show up she could share Jesus with. Right?

Not quite. Laurie knew (after years of experience) that "a little" popcorn would not feed thousands of people. And that Radius did not have the budget to supply soda to thousands of Columbians. That was actually the reason why her hands up to her forearms were stained a cherry pink color. She was stirring a ridiculous amount of Kool-Aid in a five-gallon dispenser with her homemade wooden paddle Lin (her husband) had made for her.

Yes, it was a *paddle*.

The Kool-Aid line seemed almost infinite as waves of people moved from where they were sitting and watching "The Incredibles" on the enormous projector screen and came to grab free Kool-Aid and popcorn as Laurie and her friends worked tirelessly. Strike that. They were definitely tired.

It was nearly midnight, and the movie was wrapping up. Lin and some of the other guys were putting up the three movie theatre popcorn poppers that had been popping popcorn since hours before the movie started. Some of the other Radius leaders were still conversing and meeting new people who were pleasantly surprised all this was free of charge. Andy Ott and Duncan Pleming were getting ready to take down and pack up the massive projector. Cortney Seeby and Amanda Khalil were putting up the hose they had used to make the Kool-Aid.

Yes, they used a *hose*.

Laurie smiled as a middle-school boy held up his cup for a refill. The diversity in the park was incredible. Young children, college students, older folks, homeless people, doctors, families, single guys and girls. And all of them were being exposed to the generosity of the Church. Capital **C** Church, not just Radius.

"This wasn't about shouting 'RADIUS'" and stamping that all over these people. This was about meeting people where they were," and this was about "being innovative to serve people." The crazy ideas weren't (and aren't) just for a show, but to build a culture within the body of Radius which promoted actively serving others.

Laurie, Becca Jones, Laura Player, Heidi Bozard, Alexa Stillwell, Jonathan Patton—they weren't serving just to get more people to come to their church. They were serving that the Church might be made known to more people.

And none of them were being paid.

....

So Radius Church, which had recently merged their Jammin' Java campus and their Oasis campus to form one body at Midway Elementary School, became known in Lexington and Columbia for their generosity. They had little money—most of Radius comprised of college students, young singles just embarking on careers, or young couples just starting their families. Money was not exactly flowing.

Even still, Radius put on event after event...

NEWSPAPERS: When still at Oasis, the church bought and handed out newspapers for free for months. From 2003 into 2004 Oasis leaders would wake up early on Saturdays and grab a couple cars to drive to houses neighboring the church building. One person driving, one person folding the papers, and two running alongside the car distributing the newspapers on either side. Or one person (my dad, John) driving with a couple elementary and middle school boys (my big bros) in the back of our purple minivan, sliding doors wide open as they bolted from the car, chucked papers onto a bunch of random porches, and sprinted back. Both were effective.

PARADES: In the early days of Radius, we began serving at numerous parades. On St. Patrick's Day, for example, John Reeves once decided to buy 4,000 Mountain Dews (cuz why not, right?). Some of the other Radius leaders would then hoist little wading swimming pools in the back of the trailer and fill them with ice. Chris Seeby would roll forward in his pickup truck, volunteers scrambling to snatch freezing cold drinks, handing them to anyone and everyone watching the parade. It took a lot of convincing for people to believe that the drinks were actually free—a *lot* of convincing. So, being the innovative problem solvers that Radius men are known to be, they created t-shirts for future parades with big bold letters across the chest: "Really, it's free!"

The Radius women would later discontinue these shirts.

ROSES: Radius tends to go all out for Valentine's Day and Mother's Day, and on one particular Valentine's Day, Radius Church purchased thousands of roses that groups (stationed in parking lots and intersections) handed out to women. However, they happened to do this in front of a BI-LO... which happened to be right beside a florist's shop... the owner of which happened to know Chris Seeby... you can imagine how that went down.

BAPTISMS: Everything in this book—the events, the celebrations, the difficulties, the Sunday services, the moves, the church plants—came to pass because some young men and women received the transforming grace of Jesus Christ, and they were called to share that grace. And Baptism is the symbol of this grace being received; in other words, it was (and still is) a symbol that all those crazy efforts were entirely worthwhile. This is the only place where I will mention Baptisms, and I wish I could name all of them. Stories of a father returning home from military leave to baptize his adult son. Stories of husbands embracing their baptized wives after years of prayer. Stories of high school kids convincing their parents to come to church and leading them to baptism. Stories of men and women saved from drugs, alcohol, sexual sin, grief, loss, anxiety, and trauma who have met Jesus and proclaim that He is greater than anything they have experienced before.

Those stories, those lives redeemed by Jesus, *that's* what this is all for. Those are the real stories we want you to know.

Radius—and many other churches—have given out roses, or newspapers, or mountain dews, or free popcorn, or nice conversations at the ballfield, or who knows what else in the hope that these little free gifts would be a gateway to the ultimate free gift. That these little tastes of light and generosity would arouse a deeper hunger for the true Light. So when John Reeves filled the family popcorn bowl (which happens to be very large) with $5 bills and passed it around on a Sunday morning for the members of Radius to take money and use it in their own communities; or even when our folks would give $20 tips to waiters and waitresses after Sunday services, they were trying to do life *with* each other and *with* the community *for* Christ. The purpose of these events wasn't just to put on an event—it was to be generous to the community, shining the transforming grace of the Gospel in unexpected places.

....

Though the body of believers was small, word of these sorts of life-changing stories and spontaneous events was spreading. In fact, "most people knew *about* Radius but didn't know where we met."

And through constantly serving together, Radius's core group was becoming uniquely close and interconnected. Like literally... it seemed half of the leaders had met and married at Radius by this point (I'll get you the full list later).

This foundation of leaders was constantly serving together, praying together, and attending "HD Meetings," allowing for the formation of *intimate* relationships within the small church.

Stories of God's movement, prodding, and provision were piling up. Stories similar to Andy's.

Andy in HD

Twenty-four-year old Andy Ott and his wife, Lannie Ott, began coming to Radius in the Spring of 2004. He first visited to complete an assignment for one of his classes at Columbia International University: write a paper on church-planting. Who knew he would be helping plant churches for the next twenty years?

Andy quickly immersed himself into the Radius family and went straight to work on the soundboards and technology (where he still works today); and Lannie, a sensational singer, was quickly pulled into the Radius band (where she still sings today).

In no time, they were deeply embedded into the Radius leadership, and began coming to the "HD" meetings (back when "High-Definition" was actually cool).

....

Andy and Lannie Ott pulled up to Chris and Cortney Seeby's house, entering what they affectionately dubbed the "upper room," which was a sparsely furnished bonus room above the Seeby's garage. Andy and Lannie were nearly an hour early today—but they weren't the first ones there. Sarah Ashlin Pleming was already in deep conversation with Cortney Seeby and Becca Jones, and Chris Seeby was sharing some outrageous story with Michael Beres as they sat against the opposite wall.

The evening progressed in typical fashion. When 6:30 came around, the "meeting" part of the night began. No one except John Reeves ever knew what the "meeting" would look like on a given night. And if you know John, you know that he never had much of a plan anyway.

"Alright," John opened up as the chatting died down, "someone tell me a story from the last seven days where you served one of your neighbors."

John was a nice guy, for sure, but his tone at these meetings was on another level. He expected everyone to arrive with a story about some interaction they had with the community, with other believers, and with God "in the last seven days." Not in the last month. Not two weeks. Seven days.

To everyone's relief, John turned to ask Cheryl to go first. She always seemed to have some story of meeting neighbors while she walked, or baking banana bread (her banana bread was *incredible*) and bringing her kids to deliver them to her neighborhood, or hosting families at her home.

After her a girl attending USC piped up—Kimberly? Kim? Then Jonathan Patton told a story. Then Laura Player. Then another. And another. And another. Andy eventually took his turn, and when he was finished, John suddenly asked Jeremiah Jones to pull out his guitar so they could worship some.

This wasn't out of the ordinary, though. Everyone had gotten used to the unplanned singing. They worshiped obnoxiously together in that upper room, Andy always relieved to have Lannie's beautiful voice could cover up his, well, *less* beautiful voice.

After a few songs, John instructed everyone to break up into small groups and pray for three neighbors by name. They did this nearly every time they met, and these prayers became emotional quickly. But before Andy could get *too* emotional, they were changing gears, and John was asking them to pray over each other. Crammed in that room, sweating because the AC couldn't ever keep up, talking over multiple voices, most of the groups (including Andy's) sitting on the floor— "it was awesome."

It was also emotionally draining. John formed the mood with constant intensity through the stories and the worship and the prayer. None of it could be taken lightly, and tonight especially, Andy felt God placing something on his heart. Something he wanted to discuss with Lannie immediately...

After more prayer, a few more songs, and a handful of stories, the meeting concluded and they were "dismissed," (a.k.a. they had an hour or two left for dessert and socializing in the kitchen downstairs). Somehow, Andy managed to get both Lannie and himself out the door. They hopped into their car and began buckling their seat belts.

Andy suddenly glanced over at his wife, eager to say what had been on his heart all night. "I think we're supposed to sell our house and move closer."

She looked up. "I had that same feeling tonight."

And that was it. The Otts called a realtor friend the next morning and started the process.

....

Looking back on the decision, Andy explained that "[there was] not really a discussion or a need to pray about it more. It just seemed like God had said to move and we were going to be obedient."

And they were certainly obedient. In fact, not long after Lannie and Andy sold their house in Northeast Columbia (May of 2005) and bought one in Irmo, Andy felt called to resign from his job at CIU and began working with Radius. After seeking counsel, Andy decided that he would "mail letters to 50 folks" asking for support—similar to a missionary—for one full year as he worked for Radius (as he was not being paid...). In early July of 2005, he gave his three-week notice, though only half of his needed funds were accounted for.

Nine months later, Andy found that one of his supporters was unable to send their fourth quarter check (June-August). That Tuesday Andy sat down at a staff meeting with John Reeves, Jeremiah Jones, and Chris Alford, informing them that this would be his last meeting unless God did something miraculous. They prayed for a time, and Andy found himself back in his car. I'll let him tell the rest...

"When I got home after that meeting I pulled in the driveway - content to start interviewing for other jobs - but I put my head down on my steering wheel and told God, 'I'm pretty sure you asked me to do this for a year and we're only 9 months in. I need a clear sign You want me to move on or to stay.' When I got out of the car, I went to check the mailbox. The top piece of mail was a 'security' envelope and inside was a check from someone else who had received my letters previously and wanted to support us. It was for the amount that we would have been short from the other supporter who couldn't help. All that to say, it was a crazy year of watching God do immeasurably more than I could ever ask or think."

....

I share Andy Ott's story not because it's the only story like this, but because it's a story you might hear in many of Radius leaders' early involvement with the church. The tension, anxiety, and pressure he and Lannie felt in being called by God to serve this church plant could be seen concurrently in many of the others.

This was a period of constant change and risk for the families who were working with Radius. A few of the elders at Radius noted that several of the leaders "walked away from lucrative careers" to work with the church—careers that would have paid two, three, even four times more.

But this was how the identity of Radius was formed. They wanted to hold out everything they owned with "open hands," knowing it was not theirs to keep.

And God blessed their endeavors. Radius gradually grew in size and in depth as the church solidified its core values and set its DNA. Every week, the leaders of Radius would wake up early and pray over the church. Every week, they worshiped. Every week, they set up bread and juice for communion, which has been a strong conviction of Radius from the beginning.

> **SIDE-NOTE: One Sunday they didn't have grape juice or bread, but Radius was so set on offering communion that *Dr. Pepper and doughnuts* were used as substitute.**

Every week, the leaders met and prayed. Every week, they went out to lunch and met with newcomers (meanwhile, we—the kids—would eat our Bellacino's pizza and then go outside to chuck tennis balls... or gravel... for an hour or two). As unorganized as Radius might have seemed, they were extremely disciplined. And they were learning to impact their neighbors in whatever way possible. The simple act of sitting down and having a meal with someone who wants to know about Jesus became an integral expectation for the body of believers. If you were a believer and a part of Radius, you were responsible to pour the Gospel into the lives of those around you.

When asked why they chose to stay at Radius, the vast majority of interviewees each gave roughly the same answer: "We were really seeing people's lives change," and, "the people coming to Radius actually wanted to be there."

Part 2: Sundays and "I think you're wrong"

Fun fact: after I finished the book and had my Dad read it, he had to tell me, "you barely even mentioned Sunday services at Midway." Not my fault.

Nobody really talked about them.

In fact, as I looked back through the interview notes I took, I could hardly find references to particular sermons or Sundays. And even the Sundays people did remember (i.e. that time when Radius handed out 1,000 Otis Spunkmeyer cookies for people to give to their neighbors), it was less about the Sunday and more about the stories it produced.

Nevertheless, it would be a pity if I didn't share a glimpse of what Radius volunteers and staff did for *seven years*. So here you go...

Sundays

Midway Elementary would open at 7 a.m. on Sundays, and from there it was a dead sprint.

Guys like Andy Ott and Duncan Pleming and Salim Khalil and Tim Seeby would hustle to set up sound consoles, both Mac computers (back then they had to use two different computers for lyrics and backgrounds), 75-foot extension cords, drum sets, projector screens, and speakers and amps before getting ready for sound check with the band.

Meanwhile, in front of them Pete Murphy and a crew of others would set up tables and chairs that Radius was given ("we didn't have money for anything... all we had was just stuff we found") in Pete's perfect diagram. The dude "used to measure where the chairs went" each week.

Ladies like Tina Butterfield (who even now, *over a decade* later, leads our SERVE Team at Radius Lexington!), Cortney Seeby, Amanda Khalil, and a variety of others also led the charge in setting up the kids areas, greeting teams, and the café (my personal favorite—I think I averaged somewhere between 8 and 12 powdered doughnuts a Sunday).

Every single week. Volunteers would wake up at 5 or 6 on their day off to set up. And then they would wait around to tear down afterward...

But it was during this time that Radius really solidified much of its identity. The weekly communion and worship were heavily emphasized. "People would sing like crazy." Week in and week out Jeremiah Jones, Cheryl Reeves, Lannie Ott, and the band would lead everyone in worship singing "six or seven songs each Sunday."

And you thought we sing a lot now.

After the service there was a ton of talking and greeting and catching up—my brothers and I used to roam the woods behind Midway Elementary every Sunday waiting for mom to finish her standard hourlong (give or take a few minutes) conversation.

At the same time, each week all the chairs had to be stacked and placed in the Midway closet (that closet was a huge blessing); all the sound equipment had to be taken out (even in the summers because it was needed for Movies in the Park); and all the kids supplies, tables, projectors, band equipment, et cetera had to be put up.

And then all the volunteers and leaders would go out to eat together.

....

So Sundays were both a lot of work and a lot of fun. Through the common purpose and exertion, the already tight bonds and community at Radius only grew deeper.

Which is probably why it hurt so bad when one family felt the call to leave.

As noted at the end of Part 1, Radius Church was built off the belief that this stuff we "have" is not our own. It's His. With that belief comes a lot of freedom. It's fun to be able to give and worship freely, and to be open-handed with the things that the Lord has given us.

But this belief also means we do hard things, things for the Kingdom of God that others (and even we ourselves) may not understand.

Another Move...

Cheryl Reeves and her little troop had taken the day to drive up to Easley, South Carolina to help clean up Matt and Jenny Reeves' yard, which had taken a hit from a storm earlier that week in January of 2006. Her six children were spread across the grounds, grabbing debris and entertaining themselves in the process ("bet you can't throw that stick into the wheelbarrow from there!"). John was there too, working on the other side of the yard.

Her mind reeled as she snatched another branch. For months, John and Cheryl had dreamed about possibly planting a new church in downtown Columbia, and they had been searching diligently for a home in that area. They had looked at houses, schools, neighborhoods… nothing felt right. In fact, it all felt very *wrong*.

But now, as she worked, Cheryl sensed an unexplainable pull (a pull she had felt several times before) for her family to live *here*—and not in Columbia.

It was an uneasy prospect, thinking about moving… again. Coping with change had never been Cheryl's greatest talent, but she happened to have married John Reeves, which meant immense change was almost becoming routine.

Still, moving would be extremely difficult. Six kids, ages 3-14, five of whom would be attending school. But Cheryl couldn't shake this supernatural feeling she felt…

Hours later, the kids clambered over each other to get situated in their gray suburban, and John started up the car. After a few minutes, the kids completely exhausted and nearly asleep, Cheryl looked over at John as he drove.

"I really think we're supposed to move here," she said, examining his face carefully. Not sure how he might respond.

He returned her look, perplexed. "I was just about to tell you the same thing."

………

After a few weeks of earnest prayer, the Reeves only found their confidence in their decision to move growing stronger—and John decided to break the news to the Radius leaders.

They were moving to Greenville.

The task was "excruciating," but John explained how he felt the hand of God, and that he was confident he was being told to move to Easley, South Carolina, where he would begin planting another church.

"I think you're wrong," was Chris Seeby's immediate response.

John had only been there for three years, and Radius was still very, *very* young. More importantly, Radius had no leader to replace John if he left.

The news hit others hard too. Brian and Trisha Kirkland, for instance, had just moved from Illinois to come and help at Radius—primarily because they had served with John and Cheryl and some of the others in several earlier church plants.

Even so, some of those who had served with the Reeves before were actually pleasantly surprised they had stayed in one place for a whole *three years* (trust me, it's rarely that long). Salim and Amanda Khalil remembered being unshocked by the Reeves' decision, though saddened by the prospect of losing some of their best friends and mentors.

Ultimately, that was the biggest blow. There was an "indescribable bond" between each of these men and women who served, and laughed, and wept, and shared late nights, and worked early mornings, and "gave birth to a church"—the pains of birth only deepening their bond. Not only were they losing their leadership, but they were losing their companionship. And it hurt.

Brian Kirkland, Michael Beres, Lin Keesey, and Jeremiah Jones sat down with John as he explained what he felt God wanted him to do. After praying together for much of the meeting, the elders confirmed the decision to send off the Reeves family. In the end, John, the elders, and everyone else involved knew that our relationship and mission with the Father takes precedence over our relationships with friends, and that we are not called to live a life of comfort. We are called by God to live for Him.

So Radius prepared to send off its primary leaders, wondering who God might choose to fill their shoes.

Buying a Building

Now I bet when you saw that little subtitle you thought, "Oh, Radius is actually gonna get out of that public school and get their own building." Wrong. You're like five years early. But I'll give you partial credit because technically Radius *did* buy a building—they just didn't use it.

....

John Reeves was driving around downtown Greenville with his younger brother, Matt Reeves. Not long ago, he had been led to believe that Radius Greenville (the not-yet-started church plant) would be able to share another church's building and use it for Sunday nights.

Nope. Not anymore.

It was 8:30 at night, and the two brothers' frustration was mounting. They *had* a plan. Now they needed a building fast.

That's when they stumbled upon a "FOR SALE" sign in front of the former Central Baptist Church. Without hesitation, Matt Reeves dialed up the realtor number on the sign—and despite the time, a woman picked up on the other end.

When asked how much the building was selling for, the realtor replied, "$450,000."

Matt's immediate response: "We'll take it."

....

They got a building. Great. Awesome. Only where on earth were they gonna come up with $60,000 for a down-payment?! Not to mention the little issue of finding all this money in *one month*.

Believing this building was a golden opportunity for a church plant in Greenville, John went to Radius Church in Lexington to ask the elders for money to help pay for that building. By the end of a month (after the bank surprisingly approved the offer), John returned with *$50,000* from the people of Radius Lexington, and Matt Reeves came up with the other $10,000.

> SIDE-NOTE: The $50,000 came about in some crazy ways. Dad remembered a very young newlywed couple who gave $1000 for the building. Then they came to our house late the same night... and were convicted to give *another* $1000.

Radius Church in Lexington was not only willing to give up the Reeves family as they moved to Greenville, but they *sponsored* their leave and *paid* for the new church building in Greenville when they didn't have a building of their own.

Crazy Generous.

The years 2004-2007 represented a time of foundational growth for Radius Church. As leadership changes came into play, several younger men bore greater weight in the

church. One of the interviewees described this as a time of "whiplash" for members and leaders alike at Radius—who were functioning at an incredibly fast pace without much infrastructure.

Innovate (2007-2009)

Part 1: "Faith and Fear"

A lot of people hear the word *faith* and immediately think of that feeling you get when you're in the shoe store and grandma's buying. You're excited. You're happy. You're in good hands.

But faith is much more than a felicitous feeling. There's a side of faith that is delivered to your door wrapped in fear, anxiety, and doubt. There's a side of faith that forces you to trust with everything you are. "A side that nobody sees."

Big Plans (June 2008)

Todd Carnes was an active dude. He didn't like standing around, waiting for the next thing to happen. Maybe that was why he and his wife, Kerri, had spent two years in Russia, serving as missionaries.

Then they got kicked out. A few years later they were *blacklisted* from overseas mission work throughout Central Asia in 2005. And now Todd was here, in Lexington, South Carolina. He was restless.

Todd was serving a church in the area, but his heart was searching for something more. He wanted to play a new role in changing lives—where he could speak the truth

God was laying on his heart. He was weary of routine and wanted something that would stretch his faith, something outside-the-box. And he began ruminating on the idea of church-planting...

As a result, Todd was referred (time and time again) to another leader in Lexington who was that "outside-the-box" kinda guy, and who was an experienced, successful church-planter: John Reeves.

They met for the first time at an Atlanta Bread Company in West Columbia. After introductions and some small talk, Todd began sharing his ideas for a church-plant he called "The Point." He had already gathered a small group of his trusted friends, brainstorming logistics and dreaming of a future.

After Todd finished explaining his plan, John gave him a shocking response: "When you're ready to plant a church in Lexington, we'll help you. We have some folks who really love Lexington and we'll send them with you to help you get started."

Todd was taken aback. Radius Church had a tiny budget, and a small body. But they were willing to give away their own *people* and *money* to another church! It was nuts. It was so unusual. It was, in many ways, attractive...

> SIDE-NOTE: When it says "tiny budget," it might be better translated as *"no* budget." This was a time when Radius prayed for *a week* whether to buy Jeremiah Jones a laptop for worship and graphic design. And this was the same year Salim Khalil had worked to get Radius out of debt... that's probably why this was also the year they began having "Financial Peace University" on Sunday mornings. Radius never passed a plate—and while at Oasis, their giving container was actually a Nike shoe box, size 13.

Big Risks (July 2008)

Todd Carnes was laying on the floor of his living room. Kerri and their three girls had left to visit family in Michigan, and just a few days after resigning from his former position as pastor he found himself alone in his house. For a while now, he had felt the Lord's prodding to resign, to willingly go unemployed, and to take the risk of planting a new church. Even so, "a mixture of faith and fear" filled him as he lay face-down, praying fervently.

"Is this your plan, God... or is it my plan? How in the world is this going to work out?" Right about this time, Kerri called—she was in tears when she told him she hadn't received the job she had applied for. The call ended, and more questions bounced relentlessly in Todd's head as he scrambled to figure out how he was going to provide for his family *and* plant a church. He could feel his blood pressure rising as the weight of his decision washed over him.

He knew it was time to be faithful and trust the Lord. He knew he wasn't being used for God in the way he was equipped. He knew he was being called to resign and begin the next chapter in his walk. But with no job and only two months' worth of savings, he *didn't* know how he would make ends meet.

And Todd Carnes lay there on that living room floor, his faith waging war with his anxiety as he fought to trust God for provision.

....

In less than 24 hours Todd Carnes found two separate checks in the mail—each for $27,000 from a couple who believed in his ministry and chose to support him in an *extraordinary* way. Todd was mostly relieved; he could allow himself to breathe now. But he was also reinvigorated by this radical act of generosity.

So the Carnes first utilized this money by writing two checks for two grand each—one for CrossPoint Church in Clemson and one for Radius Church in Lexington, the two churches that had offered them support in their ministry.

And the two $27,000 checks from this brother and sister in Christ supported the Carnes for the next year.

....

As the Lord worked miraculously in Todd's life, convicting him to resign at his former job while not knowing what kind of ministry he would take on, Radius Church in Lexington was struggling to find a new leader to replace John. Each week, John was making the four-hour round trip to speak at Radius in Lexington on Sunday mornings and then at Radius in Greenville on Sunday nights. And every Wednesday morning he would leave his house at 4 a.m. to spend the day in Lexington. Constantly pressed for time, John was not able to lead as he had in the past at Radius in Lexington. To counter this, men like Brian Kirkland, Lin Keesey, Jeremiah Jones, and Chris Seeby stepped up to the mound and took charge in discipleship, mentoring, pastoring, shepherding, and leading the church. Chris Alford in particular served to help with the preaching and leadership of Radius.

But even with all these men rising up, they were still badly missing a crucial piece: a singular leader. They needed someone to communicate their vision week in and week out. Someone who was prepared to lead a church.

It was a good thing God had set that someone right in front of them.

……

Guinea Worms

Kerri Carnes was generally very confident in her husband's messages. But this was one of those she just wasn't so sure about. It was hit or miss. And Kerri was really hoping it wasn't going to be a miss.

Her husband was up at the front of Radius Church, glancing over at the projector screen as he readied himself for his message. His topic: **Thou shalt not commit adultery**. You know, the typical kind of sermon you give when you're first introducing yourself to a church. Only Todd.

He was starting to speak now, and Kerri felt herself leaning forward in her seat. That's when he started describing a guinea worm—a disgusting hidden parasite that eats away the inside of your body until it becomes so large it pops out of your leg.

The screen flashed with an image, and Kerri resisted the urge to look away. Todd had made a horrific collage of gruesome photos depicting the mutilating effects of guinea worms. The audience squirmed in their seats. Kerri thought she might have heard someone squeal.

Perfect, she thought. *They'll definitely ask you back now, Todd.*

But as they left Midway Elementary that Sunday morning in July of 2008, Kerri found that Todd was as excited as she had seen him in a long time. He had been so free on that stage; he didn't have to "tip toe" or soften his words. He was able to teach that hidden sin will never stay hidden. It is too infectious, disgusting, egregious to remain contained. It will always find a way to display itself publicly.

Lord knows they weren't going to forget that anytime soon.

Later that night, after the kids were all in their rooms and ready for bed, Todd made that dangerous kind of eye contact that Kerri immediately knew meant something serious had happened.

"I got a call today..." He began. Oh boy. That was always an interesting way to begin a conversation. Kerri held her breath as he explained.

Turns out, Todd had received a job offer from another, much more established church in the area—on the very day he had spoken his first message at Radius. But Todd had quickly decided to decline.

His reasoning: "I could never have preached that sermon at this other church. And I had not risked everything me and my family owned to do something safe. I took the risk to make sure whatever we did required real faith to meet the challenges of real life."

Now there was no turning back.

....

After a period of several months, the elders at Radius in Lexington asked Todd to be Lead Pastor, despite the guinea worm sermon. Thus, John and Cheryl Reeves exited the front stage at Radius in Lexington, and Todd and Kerri Carnes entered. Todd Carnes had made up his mind that his calling was to join Radius in starting something new in Lexington, something that would stretch his faith and the faith of others. And so he declined a much more stable, well-paying job offer to accept the responsibility of leading Radius into its new future. He and Kerri leaned on the provision of the Lord and strapped themselves into the front seat of the Radius rollercoaster ride for the next eight years.

Part 2: "Arranged Marriage #2"

Marriage is a big part of the Church—and a huge part of the history of Radius. I mean, just think about it: Jeremiah and Becca Jones, Todd and Kim Lyle, Duncan and Sarah Ashlin Pleming, Jonathan and Anne Patton, Matt and Heather Jones, Steven and Heidi Bozard, Travis and Lil Mason, Alexis and Kirby Langley, Mark and Kelli Anthony **ALL** met their spouses at Radius when it was at Jammin' Java and Oasis (that's a span of barely a year when their church only consisted of about a hundred people). Obviously, Radius hasn't been bad at match-making.

Just to clarify: I'm not telling you "hey, come to Radius and find your dream girl or guy!" No. I'm simply informing you that Radius is well-acquainted with the prospect of marriage (did I mention that I'm single?).

But it's one thing to *choose* the person you want to marry, and it's quite another to have that person *chosen* for you. That's kinda how Radius Church felt when Todd Carnes came on the scene. This new guy wasn't the pastor, the leader, the friend that John Reeves had been to them for the last five years—he was just, well, new.

And people generally have a tough time accepting new.

Scarborough Cafe (2008)

Kim Lyle was hungry and very, very pregnant.

Bad combo.

Her husband, Todd Lyle (whom she met at Jammin' Java), was just pulling into Scarborough Cafe in Lexington, SC, where they were set to have a meeting with some of the new leaders of Radius. The Todd Carnes guy who was supposed to replace John had brought together some men and women that were coming to Radius with him. But Kim wasn't really in the mood to meet new people. Then again, maybe she was just hungry—it was dinnertime, after all. Some food might cheer her up.

Kim entered Scarborough Cafe behind her husband and felt a sudden impulse to cry. Or maybe throw something.

The restaurant was closed. It was just a convenient meeting place. Translation: no food.

For the next half hour Kim attempted to compose herself as the little brainstorming session broke off in a million different avenues. Ideas, opinions, and random suggestions were hurled across the table where the leaders, new and old, gathered. There was little direction in the discussion, and even less chemistry.

Kim found herself more and more disappointed with the situation as it became clear that Radius was going to completely and unreservedly focus on the Lexington community. For several of the believers who discovered their faith at Jammin' Java in downtown Columbia, this was a tough blow. Their hearts were still deeply embedded in that community...

So Kim and Todd Lyle, annoyed, saddened, and hangry, left the meeting early with several other families.

And they grabbed a bite to eat.

....

Quick spoiler alert: Todd and Kim Lyle did not remain irritated with Todd Carnes and the additional leadership added to Radius's body. In fact, Todd Lyle and Todd Carnes are now very close friends (and have even started a business together). Ultimately, the Carnes managed to battle the skepticism of strangers and friends alike as they quickly became integral leaders at Radius. Looking back, several of the Radius families noted that Todd was "exactly what [the church] needed at that time." Obviously, this is not to say that everyone was happy and there were rainbows and sunshine in the auditorium on Sundays. Things changed, and change is tough.

As worship leader, Jeremiah Jones had to adapt to Todd's schedule and organizational tendencies. As a body, the church of Radius had to get used to new philosophy, teaching style, and service layout. Elders who had previously built deep relationships with John were forced to construct an entirely new relationship with Todd (who happens to have a vastly different personality). Moreover, Kim's protests were similar to many of the believers from Jammin' Java, who still had a passion to serve in Columbia. When Todd Carnes came, this hopeful vision was more or less dissolved, and Radius looked to exert its efforts in Lexington alone.

But even as Todd Carnes was pulling in the new, John Reeves was pushing the old. The two leaders used all their leverage to compel their people toward a common vision for their church—and both groups bought into that vision quickly. In fact, a few years later Kim Lyle joined the Radius staff under Todd, where she continues to serve to this day.

If Radius Church was really going to continue to grow, it needed more stability, more structure, more vision.

In other words, more of Todd's gifting.

Part 3: "The Party Church"

When Todd and Kerri Carnes, Jerry and Allison Dominic, and Wayne and Annalee Jewell arrived at Radius, you might tend to think that they would do away with the fun, free atmosphere and insert more rigid structure... Structure, yes. Anti-fun, no. In fact, Radius became known for their big events, their "parties."

"People began calling us the Party Church."

Radius did things that made people uncomfortable. Things like having people over for parties after church—or *before* church. Things like Field Days and Slip n Slides and Jeep Pullings on Sundays. Things like outdoor baptisms in forty-degree weather and giving away 100 $100 Bills on a Sunday morning (disclaimer: this does not happen regularly).

Radius was a non-denominational church with few traditions and an excess of random, unusual ideas. So yes, Radius was unofficially dubbed "The Party Church."

Though some people might have meant this to be insulting, I think most of the people at Radius considered this a major accomplishment.

The Parties

Tailgating: Radius Church liked fellowship, and they liked food—it only made sense to have both on Sunday mornings before church. That's why Radius began to have Tailgating Sundays. On these Sunday mornings Radius members would come in small groups and bring their own food to share. Some people went all out and brought their own grills, serving up pancakes and eggs and bacon. Some people stuck to Pop-Tarts. Either way, the body would eat and socialize outside the school, and then walk in to have their Sunday service.

Field Days: Around the same time, Radius began having field days. The church body would turn out for Jeep Pullings, Slip 'N Slide kickball, or just a huge Slip 'N Slide tarp drenched in soap and water. In this way, Radius was able to build relationships with the community, have a ton of fun, and teach children to enjoy bathing all at the same time.

100 $100 Bills: Radius gave away $10,000 on one Sunday. They made this decision spontaneously at McAlister's Deli that very Wednesday. And 100 people were suddenly held responsible to impact their radius with that money. It might sound crazy, but Radius was trying to train their members to touch the people around them. This little gift was a way for Radius to catalyze that outreach and bring a tangible lesson to each of the recipients of the $100.

"Sitting down and talking about Jesus"

Sheri Byrd had just found Jesus, and it was most beautiful thing she had ever experienced.

Recently, she had begun attending Radius, and her heart was quickly stirred by the atmosphere. People cared about Jesus, which meant they cared about her... This place was the "most comfortable place" she had felt before. They were "not afraid to be real."

She was at Radius now, turning to her left, mid-smile, to see Kerri Carnes approaching her. Sheri resisted the urge to gulp. Oh gosh. This was the pastor's wife.

She regained composure and mustered a smile as Kerri came up alongside her and introduced herself. Then the most surprising thing happened—they *talked*.

"Maybe that sounds silly," but Sheri was genuinely surprised that Kerri (a pastor's wife) would have such a down-to-earth conversation with her. There was no hidden meaning behind Kerri's smile or judgement in her words. Kerri was simply interested in Sheri's life. And when Kerri asked for her number and if she wanted to grab lunch sometime, Sheri was happy to say yes.

....

Have you ever asked someone to lunch? Have you ever gone out of your way just to *listen* to someone's story?

That right there—the concept of sitting down, having a meal, and talking with someone—was and always has been a crucial part of Radius's DNA. "Know your neighbor's name" was one of those phrases that was repeated incessantly and drilled into the body of believers from Day 1. Taking the time to have a meal with someone, to listen to what they have to say, and to care about what they have to say—*that's* the beauty of the Church.

One of the Radius elders said it best: "You can *listen* to the same message over and over again every Sunday, but when you sit with someone you can *see* their story."

So Kerri Carnes invited Sheri Byrd to grab a bite to eat. And Sheri Byrd began talking to people at her work as a hairdresser. And the expectation is that Christians will impact their areas wherever they are—in your school, at the gym, on the ballfield, at the office, in your home—because the Church grows much deeper through personal testimonies at Waffle House on a Tuesday morning than generic messages in one of a thousand seats on Sunday.

And that was the focus of Radius. They wanted to be *real people*, and to have *real faith* (hence the motto). They wanted to make real friendships and incorporate their faith into those friendships—not just on Sundays. They wanted real change in their lives because they believed in a real God.

By 2009, the new leadership was equipping Radius Church to increase in number, which meant its members had to take initiative themselves. "This wasn't gonna be a church where you bring your problems to the pastor." Members at Radius had to be involved—by now, there were simply too many people for the leaders to deal with at one time.

Radius became active in "parties" and events because they wanted to be vigilant in their community—and they wanted their members to have simple chances to serve.

Thinking back to that time one interviewee remembered, "There was so much volunteering going on. There was so much *everyone* volunteering..."

But it wasn't just about volunteering and serving *within* the church; it was about volunteering *outside* the church. It was about being real people who go to football games, wine walks, concerts, and other community events while being a light for Jesus Christ.

Vision 2012

Radius was continuing to grow, and its goals needed to grow congruently. That was what this church needed now—a vision. Something tangible they could strive for.

That's why in 2009, Todd Carnes and Jerry Dominic helped roll out what they dubbed *Vision 2012*. They set three goals. Three *monstrous* goals. They wanted to cast a vision, however implausible it may seem, and get the members at Radius Church to rally towards that vision. They wanted to "swing for the fences and see what the Lord would do."

Thus, these three goals were implemented and communicated to the body:

1) Give away $1 million
2) Have 100 small groups
3) Plant 1 church

Just like that. And all this was to be done by 2012. That was what Radius was trying to accomplish. Who knew? Maybe God would provide the resources to aid them in their goals. Resources like, say, a building...

The Lord provided Radius Church with a new leader in Todd Carnes as it transitioned in 2008. Radius became more innovative and organized in its pursual of radical generosity as it served the community and rolled out Vision 2012.

STAGE 4

Organize (2010-2011)

Part 1: "God's favor on a bunch of knuckleheads"

At the beginning of Radius Church, several ministries became more of an afterthought. Kids and Youth Ministries serve as a prime example of this. Jammin' Java literally didn't even have a children's care. Oasis was mainly comprised of *very* young couples. *Splash* (the first name for youth ministries at Radius, coined by my brothers) consisted of like eight kids.

And from 2005-2009 Kids Ministries was primarily run by Radius moms who cared about what their children's environment looked like on a Sunday morning.

"Our office was Starbucks after the kids went to bed." That's where they would plan lessons, organize volunteers, and pray for their children. It was certainly difficult—they would have to unload a whole trailer of bins that someone had to drive to Midway Elementary every Sunday. Then they would set up the gym, music room, and special needs classroom with babies on hips, toddlers hugging their legs, and elementary kids struggling to keep up and "help."

So in January of 2010, Radius decided they would actually *hire* someone full-time for Kids Ministries…

"Organized Chaos"

In 2008, Joe and Meg Pitts (newlyweds), were referred to Radius in Lexington by Stuart Fuller (who had become lead pastor at Radius in Greenville). When they arrived, Lin and Laurie Keesey greeted them and quickly ushered them into serving at Radius.

Two years later, *twenty-four-year-old* Joe Pitts was cornered in IHOP by Todd Carnes and Jerry Dominic. They asked him to be the Radius Kids Ministries Leader—ages 0-18. No, he did not have any kids himself. Yes, they asked him anyway. No, he was not offered more money, more benefits, or a better work schedule. Yes, he decided to quit his job.

Joe remembered that "it wasn't very logical."

Got that one right.

But he loved Todd. Loved Radius Church. Loved the Lord, and he and Meg thought this was what the Lord wanted them doing. Why not, right?

Thus, the fun began.

Every Sunday, the Radius Kids were (as Chris Seeby liked to call it) "breaking a sweat." There was a lot of freedom for the children, and Radius began focusing on an atmosphere of fun, letting kids play and weaving the Gospel into those times.

Meanwhile, young Joe Pitts was learning a lot of new things. For instance, Todd Carnes felt the need to sit down with Joe at one point and say, "Joe, you can't communicate to volunteer moms like you do to guys at work."

Other lessons Joe learned:

1) playing soccer in the school hallways = knocking out ceiling panes
2) breastfeeding is a real thing mothers have to do + mothers need some privacy when they do it
3) kids want to come back = parents want to come back

But for all the things Joe was learning, he was also serving to close a huge gap that Radius needed to be filled. He was implementing more vision. They were setting goals to gain X many volunteers, have X many middle or high school kids, and see X many baptisms in student ministry, which Radius had never done before.

At the same time, Joe was recruiting, and people were willing to serve. By 2012, a committed group of middle and high school group leaders (including future elders, staff members, and youth pastors) were volunteering hours of their time to lead Radius students.

The volunteers were there, and the vision was set. In the words of Joe Pitts: Radius Kids Ministries had officially improved to *"organized* chaos."

Part 2: "Oh no. What have we done?!"

It was time for change at Radius—everyone knew it. They had been holding services at Midway Elementary since 2004.

It was now 2010.

Sure, they had bought a building for Radius Church in Greenville—and sure, they were very responsible with the facilities at Midway Elementary School (cool story: the custodian [Mike] who helped Radius into the Elementary School on Sundays became a follower of Christ after years of exposure to and service for the Gospel, and still attends Radius to this day). But if they were going to continue to grow, a building was essential.

Aware of this reality, the church began fasting and praying, asking the Lord for a building. Initially, Radius set their sights on The Lite House (now Michaelis Mattress) building off Highway 1 in Lexington. They started working, planning, strategizing ways to get the building. They talked with nearby neighbors to make sure they would have enough parking. Excited about the possibility, they dove into the process of getting a permit and an approval to change the zoning.

Then things didn't work out. They got "all the way to the wire," before being rejected at the very end. Some of the neighbors had heard the rumors about Radius, the "party church," and asked that they wouldn't be given the property.

The building was off limits. And it hurt, badly. But God's plan was more than Radius could have anticipated—and He was working even in the midst of their disappointment.

Soon enough, "God put something in [Radius's] path that [they] couldn't even fathom." It happened to be a big box of a building that was formerly an Ace Hardware located in downtown Lexington. The leaders of Radius fasted and prayed before the auction, earnestly asking God to provide them with a chance to get the building. At one point, Todd even remembered being led to that empty building by a good friend of his who was "a man of great faith." Todd's friend "was raising his hands and praying in a loud voice and made [Todd] raise [his] hands in the middle of the parking lot to pray over the building." Even so, the appraisal for the building was $1.4 million, which pretty much meant there was absolutely no way Radius could get it.

Auction

It was a cold mid-October morning, and Todd Carnes kept checking his phone to make sure his contact hadn't texted or called him in the last twelve seconds. Nope, he hadn't.

Todd was standing outside the building he hoped might be used for Radius Church in the near future. He was attending an auction—which was about as familiar to him as ballet—and he was getting anxious. Todd's friend was supposed to be here, guiding him through the process, helping him understand this whole auctioning thing.

But he hadn't shown up.

Todd gave another quick glance at his phone. Nothing.

That's when the auctioneer started hollering, quieting the crowd and commanding their attention. He let them know that the auction was about to begin. Todd was alone.

As time went on, the bids rose steadily, Todd's stomach was churning faster and faster. His budget was $700,000—only *half* of that 1.4 million appraisal—as Radius had only come up with $70,000 for the down-payment. But things were looking up. By the time the bidding reached $500,000, there were only two bidders left (including Todd). They started trading bids by the thousand, then by a couple hundred... and finally the man dropped out.

Todd had gotten the building for $616,000.

Despite his friend's absence (turns out he was extremely sick that morning), Todd was able to score an amazing deal. After all the prayer, fasting, dreaming, and researching, Radius Church was going to have a building. For the body of believers at Radius, it was a time where the things they were asking God "actually happened in front of [them]." They prayed, and God provided before their very eyes, granting them a functional building in an incredible location (downtown Lexington).

Now, they would all savor this moment for as long as they could.

Or at least until the next day...

Building the building

"Oh no. What have we done?" The first thought Kerri Carnes had when she walked into that trashed Ace Hardware.

There was "a lot of buyer's remorse" for the people working on the building. The place was a mess. They were literally using the old shopping carts to wheel out debris from within the building. Poles—weight-bearing poles—

needed to come out (around $30,000 just to take *one* out). An entirely new arrangement was needed to make the building functional for Sundays. Not to mention Radius still had to pay off over $500,000 more over the next few years.

In the profound words of Jerry Dominic: "It was a lot of flippin' work."

At the same time though, the building showed a ton of promise. And Radius was lucky to have an experienced builder in Wayne Jewell who worked with Jerry Dominic and *tons* of volunteer teams to lead the charge in demo, teardown, painting, and construction over the next six months.

> **SIDE-NOTE: Even as Radius prepared to move into their new building, a group of around 80 volunteers undertook a series of projects all along Main Street to serve the people near them. From raking leaves to painting signs to singing Christmas carols, Radius Church quickly introduced themselves to their new neighbors.**

Part 3: "300 Sundays"

Andy Ott came up with the term "300 Sundays," alluding to Radius's stay in Midway Elementary School. Originally, it was thought that Radius's renting of Midway would be a temporary stay—about six months or so. 30 Sundays was kinda the max.

Over 300 Sundays later, Radius was still meeting in that public school building. But on April 24, 2011, after buying the building in October and toiling to clean, tear-down, repair, reconstruct, and improve the old Ace Hardware, Radius was ready to move in for Easter Sunday.

Easter Sunday

Chris Seeby and the Radius leaders knew that their first Sunday (on Easter of 2011) would be a big day.

But they didn't know it would be *this* big.

It was "electric." There was "such anticipation" for this day that Radius had dreamed of for so long. There was such "hope that God would fill that building."

God filled it and *then some*.

Radius Church was slammed in its first service in their Ace Hardware building off Main Street. It was an emotional day for Chris and the others, who—after seven years of investment—were blown away by the "excitement with which [the community] embraced us." Chamber of Commerce officials, Town Council members, the Chief of Police, the Mayor, and many other community leaders came out in support of Radius as it began a new stage (pun intended) of its development.

That's when Chris realized he was sweating. It was hot. Like *really* hot.

Two of the HVAC units were working in reverse— blowing out heat. Typical.

The building was semi-clean. Someone had U-Hauled in 500 free chairs from a church in Charleston a week ago. The carpet had been put in last night (also U-Haul). And now the air conditioning didn't work.

But despite the heat, the morning was a beautiful, "worship-filled" meeting for the people of Radius to rejoice in the gift of the Lord. And after the service, Chris didn't hear one negative comment.

A little bit of sweat couldn't steal the excitement in that building.

....

For the last nine years, Radius has used that old Ace Hardware building to extend to thousands of people. Today, this building has approximately a 90% usage rate. Meaning 9 out of 10 days someone from the Lexington community will use the building for meetings, events, or afterschool programs.

The Lord was faithful. And Radius, a church body that was fluctuating between 300-350 members, nearly doubled overnight as 687 people packed into the "standing-room-only" auditorium.

....

So you're probably thinking "Finally! Took them long enough!" And yes, it took a really, *really* long time for Radius to get a building and establish permanence—which, in reality, can be very important for a church.

But one of the primary reasons Radius took such an extended time in acquiring a building and organizing their own kids, youth, and missions ministries was because they were generous with their finances, advocating for several other ministries outside their own...

Radius Greenville/Frazee Center

You might remember that time when John and Matt Reeves found that building in Greenville for another Radius church plant. Lexington offered up $50,000 for the down-payment, buying a building for another church when they didn't have one.

Well here's what happened as time went on:

— Radius Greenville, eventually led by Stuart Fuller, fixed up portions of that building after a few years, and continues to minister to the downtown Greenville area. It has since begun to meet in a network of community groups as it multiplies and reaches more and more of those desiring Jesus.

— Matt and Jenny Reeves led the renovation of the entire building and began an afterschool program called the Frazee Dream Center (named after James Frazee who helped plant DCF) there that has grown and touched the lives of hundreds of disadvantaged children in the Greenville area, providing opportunities for these children academically, athletically, and spiritually.

— Plus, my bros and I got to be a part of some of the best hide-and-seek games of all time. That place was like a perfect combination of haunted house/abandoned mansion/castle.

Ezekiel Ministries

Josh Whitlock was a partner with Radius when he felt called to help children in inner-city Columbia. Similar to the Frazee Center, Radius offered up resources and money to catalyze Eze Ministries' foundation. Now, Eze is led by a team of men and women who have a heart for serving children. Their mission: "to share the love and truth of Jesus to families in inner-city Columbia... by providing tangible help in the areas of education and family literacy."

Today, Ezekiel Ministries provides an afterschool program at Radius Lexington that promotes biblical truths while investing in underprivileged children's academia.

Hundreds of children in our area continue to benefit from Ezekiel Ministries.

....

Those are some of the bigger stories Radius had a part in. But I'm missing so many more. So many more beautiful moments where the church—or even an individual member—gave away their stuff to another church/group/individual because they placed themselves second. Because they were "*others-ambitious.*"

It's interesting how fondly everyone remembered those times when they were giving so many things away. They chuckled about how hard it was for them at the time, of course. But still, there's something about exhausting equal or greater *effort*, and *emotion*, and *innovation*, and *determination*, and *talent*, and even *ambition* for **others** as we do for ourselves. That ability—as difficult as it may be— is the height of love.

And the height of freedom.

After supporting several other ministries, Radius Church was finally able to buy, renovate, and move into their own building from October 2010-April 2011. As they moved into the building, Radius improved its Kids Ministries, served its new radius, and doubled in size

Establish (2011-2015)

Part 1: "Apple Pie"

I've been told that Todd Carnes used to make an analogy with "apple pie." He would say that as Christians, we don't want our life with Jesus to be one slice of pie. We don't want to have our *faith* as one piece of our pie (pie = life) while *work* is another and *family* is another and *hobbies* are another, et cetera. As believers, we need our faith to be the apples in the pie—and we need those apples to permeate every slice.

As Radius moved into their building on Main Street, it became this group of believers' mission to extend to every part of Lexington. Your office. Your football team. Your classmates. Your coworkers. Your next-door neighbors. Heck, your local Wendy's workers. Every part of your radius needed the light of Jesus.

There are way too many stories I could share from over these years in 2011-2015, but I wrote down just a few. Here's a couple things the men and women I interviewed were most excited about.

"Marcelo's Trailer"
Student Ministries knows how to do some work. I mean

honestly, the work that Radius Students have done to help others in need—it's incredible.

After helping to beautify that fixer upper of an Ace Hardware (and after watching several HGTV episodes), the Radius Students went to work again as they aided a family who spoke little English and was in danger of being evicted. Seeking to help this family, Radius began searching for trailers. The very day they began looking, someone sold them one for cheap. The trailer "fell in [their] laps."

Radius bought the family an entirely new trailer, and the Radius Students worked to landscape the property.

"Family Vacations"

Brian Kirkland was on vacation preparing his finest Bon Jovi impersonation.

The best part? Most of the Radius Staff was preparing with him, and about three hundred people in their Radius family were about to watch.

In 2013, 2014, and 2015 Brian led the Radius Family Vacation Week at a beach resort. This year (after the Bon Jovi performance, of course) he and the Radius Staff were ready for classic gigantic bingo, ridiculous karaoke competitions, smuggled ice cream, mass trivia, field days, kickball games, ultimate frisbee, and whatever else sounded like fun at the beach.

And yet for Brian (who several of the leaders at Radius called the "ultimate shepherd" and the guy who "made Radius a small group church") the beauty of those times of rest and enjoyment was that Radius was growing together; "community was at a premium." Intermixed among all the fun and games were times of deep, compelling worship and focus on God.

"Some people still say this was the best idea Radius has ever come up with."

> SIDE-NOTE: If there's anyone I wish I could've written more about, it would probably be Brian and Trisha Kirkland. It's just hard to recognize all the baptisms, Good Friday services, counseling sessions, and the subtle influence they have over the culture and community of Radius. The Radius Staff has even unofficially dubbed Brian the "Pastor of Fun." For just about as long as Radius has been around, Brian has played the primary role in crafting the atmosphere of Radius' staff and church body, bringing liveliness, community, and many, *many* practical jokes.

"Give Hope"

In 2012, Radius Church addressed a problem: they were struggling to find the best places to distribute generosity. Who were the people that *really* needed help? Seeking to answer this question, Radius decided they needed solid "community partners" to engage in the most effective "community impact." The answer to that question: schools.

Radius has always been extremely involved in the public school system. Midway Elementary, Carolina Springs Elementary, Saluda High, Rocky Creek Elementary—all locations of Radius Churches. These schools are the center of their respective communities. And "we believe that our teachers and administrators know who needs the money more than we do." So, beginning in 2013, the body at Radius has begun to donate to schools near our campuses throughout the Advent season. Checks anywhere from

$1,000 to $10,000 are donated to schools to help the children who need it the most. "Checks with no strings attached."

From 2013-2015, and from 2017-2020 Radius has run "Give Hope," a giving drive dedicated to students in need. In 2019's drive alone, the men and women at Radius along with partnering businesses gave over $200,000.

When presenting one of these checks, Andrea Krick remembered being hugged and "picked up off the ground" by a female principal at one of the schools. Todd Carnes remembered receiving a call four years after Radius had presented her school with a check; the principal could still remember exact details about how she distributed that Give Hope money to help some of the children in her school.

....

Those are just a handful of the crazy things Radius came up with to grow together as a family and to engage in their community. Not mentioned were the Mud Runs, Adoption Sundays, and Cornhole Tournaments. It was a season of fun and major outreach.

In 2015, as South Carolina experienced arguably the worst flood in its history in the wake of Hurricane Florence, Radius Church became "the hub for people in Lexington to coordinate needs." Chris Seeby led much of the coordination between organizations, teams, and work crews in Lexington for tear-down, clean-up, and repair.

In other words, by 2015, Radius had grown from six adults who loved their neighbors to nearly a thousand. Same love. Same purpose. More people. A group of ordinary people who—because of Jesus Christ—served their neighbors for *years*. And our little church body (like so many others) was able to build enough trust to be relied upon when tragedy struck.

………..

"GO!"

I've harped excessively on the ways Radius believes the Church is not a *building*, but I don't think I've done a great job at expressing how we believe the Church is not an *institution*. It's not about doing church or attending church or just being a part of our church, it's about *being* the Church. It has always been Radius's vision to inspire innovation for the sake of the Gospel, and if someone has ideas or feels called by God then they should "GO!" And several partners at Radius have done just that.

The Josh Whitlocks (founded Ezekiel Ministries), Jen Thompsons (CEO at Lighthouse for Life), and Steve and Jennifer Lorchs (Founders of Hydromissions) of the world all work outside of what one might deem "church" work (i.e. Sunday service). But in helping impoverished children, restoring sex-trafficking victims, and providing overseas communities with water, these organizations have taken their excitement for Jesus and are fighting to combat the evil and trouble of this world with love and service.

For years, each of these organizations have been partners with Radius Church in our common mission. Their passions create avenues for the body of believers to serve, and the believers can supply people and resources.

It's not about an institution. It's about *being* the Church. So if you're called, *GO!*

………..

Now, I'm going to say this again because I got a little uncomfortable (literally sweating as I type) writing some of these stories.

The purpose of writing all this stuff down is not to glorify "RADIUS." It's not about a brand or a certain church or a certain group of people. It's about encouraging both Radius members and others to see what God has done through an imperfect, weak, crazy group of individuals who want to serve Him.

Part 2: "Missions"

One of the other big developments of Radius Church from 2011-2015 was the birth of international missions through Radius Church. Until this time, Radius had not been able to sponsor missions, and had somewhat lacking connections overseas. But in just a few years, the Lord provided several new opportunities to shine His light in new territories...

Hydromissions

Picture this: you step out of the airplane and into a foreign country with half a drill and a backpack with ten days of food and clothes. You have one partner who is carrying the other half of the hydromissions drill ("a modified post hole digger"). You meet the natives. You assemble the drill and dig a well. You teach the natives how to make their own drills and wells using natural resources. An entire community has water to drink for years to come.

You're crazy. Or awesome. Or both.

But since Steve and Jennifer Lorch founded Hydromissions and developed the Explorer Hand Drilling System (EXP-50), 328 projects like this have been undertaken, helping an estimated 110,000 people in 34 different countries.

For years Radius has partnered with Hydromissions in sending folks on mission to create wells and donating to the foundation.

Mexico

Jerry Dominic had just received a call from Todd Carnes. Todd had told him that he was going on a trip to Mexico to scope out possible missions opportunities for Radius. He'd asked several other people to come on the mission trip, but they had all been unable to go. So now— after everyone else said "no"—he was asking Jerry.

Ouch.

Jerry gave one of those *oh-I'll-think-about-it* responses and hung up. But later that week Todd called again.

"So was that an actual 'I'll think about it' or not?" Todd asked point-blank.

Jerry thought it over. He had never been on a mission trip. He had three kids. He had not planned at all for this. Why not?

So Jerry and Todd flew to Mexico with a team of others (including their children, Laina and Justin) and began evangelizing in the streets. They were "accepted and rejected," driving two and a half hours in the back of a pickup truck just to talk about Jesus. "It was awesome."

Over the next few years, Radius took nearly 100 people on trips to Mexico as they preached Jesus, worked on projects, learned a little Spanish, and had a ton of fun.

Thus Radius Missions was formed.

Now, Radius has been able to send teams to Mexico, Nicaragua, El Salvador, Guatemala, India, Vietnam, and Moldova.

GEMS-India

Some time ago, Todd Carnes (and later Andy Ott) developed a partnership with a man named Stephen, who is an indigenous missionary in India. Though living on the opposite side of the globe, Stephen's passion for church-planting matched Radius's. Stephen (working with nonprofit GEMS-India) has helped to develop 67 churches, train 185 pastors, and begin a seminary in his house in India. Radius Church partners with Stephen and GEMS-India, and was able to fund St. Paul's School in India which will train children to learn English that they might escape the poverty of India.

St. Paul's School opened in 2015 with 13 students. It now has over 160.

Part 3: "Priests" and "Prophets" "Together"

If the men and women at Radius were going to have apples in every slice of their pie, they needed to be *equipped* to do this very thing. So Todd Carnes set out on a few creative, intriguing sermon series that would serve to challenge Radius to reach their neighbors.

Priest Collars

In 2012, Radius embarked on what they called the "Year of the Priest." In other words, for an entire year, Todd Carnes would repeatedly dwell upon the idea that "we are all priests" (1 Pet. 2:9), who "talk to people on behalf of God, and talk to God on behalf of people." Throughout the year, Todd began to call up people who had moved in their radius (during the Sunday morning service) and place an actual "priest collar" on them. Then their story from the week would be shared with the entire Radius body.

Dozens of stories were told. And dozens of collars were given out. This was a time for Radius to realize that it "wasn't about the guy on the stage," it was about real people with real faith. This was the exemplification of that "apple pie." People should be developing their own stories—not waiting for someone who is a "pastor" or "priest."

Soon, 2013 rolled around, and Todd decided to come up with a new series: "Year of the Prophet." It was time for genuine, heartfelt, unsoftened truth.

Radius has always been good at that stuff. Maybe a little *too* good.

"Relevant and Edgy"

"I was once told that our problem is *not* that people are hearing and rejecting it—rather they are not hearing it because they don't see it as relevant," Todd Carnes told me.

It was great if people loved what Radius had to say. It was even okay if they hated what Radius had to say. It was not okay if people were indifferent. If they ignored the message.

So we simply had to come up with a way to be relevant *and* edgy.

—*Liar, Liar*

2 Corinthians 10:5 "We destroy arguments and every lofty opinion raised against the knowledge of God, and take every thought captive to obey Christ"

"Liar, Liar" was a way of battling the lies that are proclaimed in our culture, "but are actually wolves in sheep's clothing." In other words, this series focused on lies that our culture calls *liberating truths*.

Todd began preaching sermons on societal lies: "I was born this way", "You owe me", "It is what it is", "Don't judge me, Bro!", "It's just sex", and "You are how you look." This was a practical series that supplied the members of Radius with articulate ammunition to speak out against the lies of the world.

—*I Married a Prostitute*

Hosea 1:2 "the LORD said to Hosea, "Go, take to yourself a wife of whoredom, and have children of whoredom, for the land commits great whoredom by forsaking the Lord."

It's funny how uncomfortable we are with a sermon series title like, "I Married a Prostitute," when the Bible itself is full of provocative, suggestive, and uncomfortable material. If we're being honest, the Bible is definitely rated R.

When people entered the auditorium and saw the big bold letters projected on the screens: "I Married a

Prostitute," it was pretty difficult to "just dismiss or ignore." And Radius began teaching through the story of Hosea, a man who married a prostitute in order to act out the constant faithfulness of God (our bridegroom) even when we (the adulteress) commit "great whoredom" in chasing after our own gods: sex, drugs, money, lust, possessions, power, etc.

—*Sex Ed*

Song of Solomon: Literally the whole book

Radius did a sermon series on sex. Kids Care was thriving. And in all truthfulness, "Sex Ed" became a "really fun series." The married, engaged, dating, and singles alike were able to hear God's truth on the impact of love, relationships, sex, marriage, and desire.

"Sexuality is such a powerful force in all of our lives, and it can be one of the most ecstatic, fulfilling things in our lives or one of the most depressing, destructive things in our lives." And if the Church doesn't constantly speak out the biblical truths and beauties of sex, then the world will have the lone voice on the matter.

And that's why we had Sex Ed at Radius!

"Together for the City"

In 2012 and 2013, Radius began a partnership between 8-10 churches in the town of Lexington: "Together for the City." During this movement, the churches collaborated to make T-shirts, shoot videos, and move through similar sermon series for a month out of the year. But the most special part about this partnership was when pastors would "exchange churches" for a Sunday. Meaning

Todd would go speak to another church in Lexington while the pastor at the other church would speak at Radius. A group of churches essentially switched pastors for one Sunday out of each of these years.

Though that might sound a little uncomfortable, the message that was being sent to the churches in Lexington was this: "there is only ONE church in Lexington" and we all serve the same God.

Part 4: "Moving"

Yes, I named this Part *"Moving."* Clearly I'm running out of creativity. And yet I think it's important to note that the simple act of moving houses, locations, and occupations has been of tremendous importance for Radius's story. As a kid who moved nine times across five states in my first eighteen years of life, I can attest to the sacrifice, the difficulty, and the adventure of moving for a God we cannot see. Really it's just one big, messy picture of obedience. All the stuff already written, and all the things that are to be written in the future are Radius's hopes at exalting God in whatever way He asks.

Sometimes that's a ton of fun. Sometimes it's not.

Another Move

Jeremiah Jones had been serving at Radius Church since day one. He was leading worship when it was just his guitar and voice, Cheryl Reeves' background vocals, and Duncan Pleming's djembe. He was at Jammin' Java and Oasis; he was at Midway; he made the four-hour round-trip to lead at Radius in Greenville every Sunday night for almost *five years*; and he was at the new Radius building now, leading again.

But Jeremiah and Becca Jones finally felt that the Lord was calling them elsewhere—and in 2012, they moved to Florida with their two children.

The gap left in the wake of Jeremiah's absence was enormous. He was singing upwards of 50 Sundays a year. He was an extremely talented songwriter and worship leader. And he and Becca were deeply immersed in and connected to the body from the very beginning.

Jeremiah was a friend, mentor, and brother to many of the members at Radius. The core group from Radius knew him and his walk with the Lord—they trusted him to lead them in worship.

That kind of trust can't be duplicated overnight.

For some time, Tim and Gina Lane, Mike Stratton, Lannie Ott, and Michael Hornacek helped to lead worship in Jeremiah's place as Radius searched for someone who could step in and lead the body for years to come.

After about two years, Mike Funderburk came onto the scene.

Now I'll be honest—I grew up with Jeremiah Jones leading worship for literally every Sunday ever. When I visited Radius Lexington and saw this Funder-something-or-other guy leading worship with fancy stage lights and skinny jeans, I was immediately skeptical. And it's true, similar to the transition between Todd and John, Mike wasn't going to be Jeremiah. It's impossible for someone to accrue years of trust the first time they walk on a stage.

But despite the big shoes to fill, Radius has been blessed by Mike's "integrity," "knowledge of the Bible," and incredible musical talent. Mike Funderburk has picked up where Jeremiah Jones left off, teaching the body to worship by "truly worshiping even as he leads from the front." As one of the elders from Radius told me, "that's special."

Now, in 2020, the years of trust have definitely stacked up.

> SIDE-NOTE: Don't be fooled by the skinny jeans and the cool haircuts. From what I've heard, this man is as good with a gun as he is with a guitar (and that's saying something).

White Knoll

Remember Vision 2012? Part of that vision was to plant a church. And in March of 2013 (yes, we were just a tad late), 75 members of Radius Lexington who lived in the Red Bank area were sent to begin a church plant at Carolina Springs Elementary School.

Radius White Knoll was soon underway as the Murphy's, Autry's, Hicks', Wiggins', Taylor's, Barfield's, Korey's, Bolin's, Lane's, and several other families went from Radius Lexington to Radius White Knoll and quickly took initiative in guiding their body through the first stages of its infancy. Similar to Radius in Lexington, a group of men (primarily from these families) soon began praying together one very early morning each week. They had the people and the drive.

But they still needed a leader. Excited to start and aggressive as ever, Radius had already hired someone to drive the church-plant in White Knoll. Quickly, though, it became clear that they needed someone else to lead—a more experienced church-planter...

....

I could definitely take up a few pages to write another story right here, but it's really getting redundant. SPOILER ALERT: the Reeves are moving again!!! By the summer of 2013, John Reeves was in the process of handing off another church plant in Dubuque, Iowa when he began itching to help plant Radius White Knoll. It was that same kind of stirring he and Cheryl had felt so many times before. After much prayer, though, the elders at Radius Lexington decided to keep him where he was. A few months later, they changed their mind, and in November of 2013, the elders of Radius in Lexington asked John Reeves to move back to Lexington. So we said goodbye to our friends, and to Radius Dubuque (the church plant), and moved to Red Bank, South Carolina.

The Radius family quickly reached out to us, and one family generously offered to let us stay at their home for several weeks before we found and moved into our rental house. For the record, me, Chunk, and Malachi didn't need any help unloading those two *ginormous* Penske trucks (mom is one of those people who keeps *everything*), but a slew of excited families—some of whom we had never even met—swamped us. Old friends from Lexington, and new friends from White Knoll greeted us, checked in on us, and fed us for weeks after moving.

So John Reeves and his family were introduced to the wonderful folks in White Knoll, and over the next few years the church there grew and developed a deep foundation. It became known for its generosity as it paid off the last $29,000 of Radius Dubuque's new building;

SIDE-NOTE: That building in downtown Dubuque is now not only home to another Radius Church but to an afterschool program named the "Dubuque D.R.E.A.M. Center," which offers its own athletic teams and academic tutoring to help over 150 participating children.

as it sent some of its members and resources to plant City Church in West Columbia; as it provided food for the White Knoll High School football team before every game; as it entertained hundreds for Super Bowl™ parties; as it gave away free boiled peanuts (Wes Stillinger's boiled peanuts are absolutely amazing), free meals, free landscaping, free CARS (yes, that word is supposed to be plural).

Needless to say, John and Cheryl found themselves right at home as Radius White Knoll flourished and moved in its community. But they couldn't get too comfortable. Not yet...

Radius established its name and its beliefs as it embarked on a slew of fun internal and outreach ministries while creating several intriguing sermon series to combat the culture of the day and grow in relationship with the churches of Lexington. Meanwhile, Radius focused its efforts on planting Radius White Knoll and creating Missions opportunities across the globe.

Multiply (2016-Now)

Part 1: "You *never* see that"

Todd Carnes had been coaching people to be "priests" in the marketplace for the last fifteen years. And after almost seven years of leading Radius, he began ruminating on when he might step out of his role as *"coach"* and become a *"player"* in the marketplace again. For months he contemplated this thought with the elders at Radius Lexington, and early in 2015, they decided together that Todd would continue to teach for five more months as he gradually transitioned out of his leadership role to tackle this new challenge . . . the marketplace.

By June of 2015, the transition was complete, and the Carnes family entered a new stage of their lives. For over a year afterward, Radius Lexington underwent a period of vast change as Chris Seeby and Ryan Allred stepped up as interim pastors. During this time, Radius Church in Lexington demonstrated amazing unity under the elders' leadership as several families helped to carry the weight of Todd and Kerri's absence.

Still, even with such unity, Radius needed a leader. Another visionary.

Uganda and Ex-Church Planter

John Reeves was in Uganda with Jonathan Patton (a good friend who attended Radius in Jammin' Java long ago). He had his Bible out and was just finishing up 1 Samuel. David—one of the most monumental figures in the Old Testament—was hiding in the caves from King Saul. It was John's favorite part. But it ended quickly, and John began to turn to 2 Samuel.

He didn't really like 2 Samuel. David was no longer the underdog, the warrior, the shepherd boy with several older brothers. By 2 Samuel, David had been anointed King over Israel.

That's when it hit John. For the past 20 years John had been the worker, the church-planter, the guy that gets his hands dirty.

But was David being unfaithful when he became the leader of Israel? Was David any less faithful as head of the entire nation as he was with his small flock of sheep?

John returned from Uganda with a new perspective. His identity was not in church-planting, it was in whatever the Lord wanted him to do. And he believed the Lord wanted him to make another move...

....

John returned home and met with the elders, offering to lead Radius Lexington. Offering to return to the church he had left some nine years before. Offering to step out of his role as a church-planter for the first time in over twenty years.

So if John wasn't going to be the church-planter himself, he had one primary stipulation when he took the position as Lead Pastor: one of Radius' central focuses would be to train and send *others* to plant churches. The elders were already eager to do this very thing—so they agreed and John was appointed as Lead Pastor of Radius Lexington.

Not long after, John had what he called a "really, really hard meeting with White Knoll." The Radius White Knoll Partners all sat in that elementary school cafeteria and listened as John explained that he would be preaching at both Radius Lexington *and* Radius White Knoll starting in Fall of 2016. He and his family were moving from Red Bank and closer to Radius Lexington. He could no longer be to White Knoll what he had been before.

In the ensuing months, John continued speaking at both White Knoll and Lexington. Meanwhile, Derrick Liferidge (who had actually been a part of *Oasis* in the very beginning!) began serving in various capacities with the White Knoll body. A few months later, John was already talking to Derrick about taking over the leadership at Radius White Knoll. And as time progressed, Derrick continued to develop as a communicator and leader. John faded out as Derrick and later Joe Pitts (who served as Children's Director and then Youth Pastor at Radius Lexington before moving with his family to White Knoll) eased into the leadership of the White Knoll body.

They continue to lead to this day.

Friendships

This part is something that I wanted to write. Nobody told me to write this, but I felt it crucial for you to grasp the uniqueness of Radius's leadership.

In 2008, John Reeves left center-stage because he believed that someone else could do a better job than him, and that the Lord wanted him elsewhere. Todd Carnes took that stage and guided Radius Lexington for a little less than a decade before realizing that his season of leadership was coming to a close, opening the door for his next challenge. Then John moved back into the driver's seat.

Here's the best part: Todd still comes to Radius. Todd still works with the Lead Staff Team on ideas and developments. On several occasions, Todd has *preached* at Radius.

"I loved Radius. I didn't want to go somewhere else."

Today, John Reeves and Todd Carnes are still the best of friends. The only time they really divide is when Clemson is playing Alabama (go tigers)! Cheryl Reeves and Kerri Carnes are the same way—they walk and talk *all the time.*

In a world infected with the desire for power, for popularity, for winning the competition, for being in the spotlight, God has humbled two very prideful, *very* competitive, very capable men. And because each of these men have a love for God, they are able to unite and worship Him together even now. Instead of an awkward, or contentious, or apathetic relationship that might be found when one leader exits and another enters, their common belief in Jesus Christ has given them deep trust and genuine friendship.

Through God's direction, John Reeves was able to hand the baton to Todd Carnes when he felt it was the right time, and Todd was able to hand it right back to John when *he* felt it was time.

As was best put by one of the elders: "you *never* see that happen."

Part 2: "Send your best"

So John Reeves made that whole commitment to leading Lexington and not being a church-planter and all that stuff. If you know John, though, you know that his heart for church-planting wasn't going to just die out with his new position. In fact, God has used Radius to multiply, generating more church plants in the last *four* years than it had in the *thirteen* years prior.

Radius in Lexington has often become the launching pad from which other plants have taken off into surrounding areas. The people at Radius have been excited to start their own churches in their own communities, the elders have provided guidance and vision, and John has served as a mentor, a catalyst, and a leader of these plants.

Saluda

Ben and Holly Harrison began driving from Saluda to attend Radius Church nearly five years ago. The couple soon found themselves inviting friends from Saluda to Radius, and they all made that forty-five-minute drive to church each Sunday. Soon enough, the Radius members from Saluda formed their own small group—meeting and discussing what it meant to serve their radius.

But to this group of believers, it seemed counterintuitive to drive nearly an hour just to talk about impacting their area. And in 2015, they decided (as a group of about fifteen) to begin a church plant out of Saluda.

For almost a year, these men and women in Saluda gathered as a church on Sunday nights. But up to that point Radius Saluda was dependent on the help of Chris Seeby, John Reeves, and Michael Funderburk for teaching, worship, and administration. They needed a leader—more specifically, a church-planter.

That year, God brought Ross Kellis out of where he was serving in Africa to come be that church-planter. Talk about networking.

So in January of 2016, Ross and his wife Heather came onto the scene. And by February, Ross began praying for another leader—someone who could help Radius Saluda with its efforts to diversify its body.

One week later Albert Etheridge showed up.

God was obviously moving, and moving quickly.

Over the past few years, Radius Saluda has displayed an *incredible* outreach for its community. It has initiated "Serve Saluda," which was created first to be a weeklong service project in the summer. Radius (especially Radius *students* from other campuses) has helped its neighbors repair, rebuild, and clean-up others' houses, property, or businesses to improve the Saluda community.

But after leaving such an impression on the community, "Serve Saluda" has become more of a yearlong process. Volunteers from Radius Saluda work on "at least one large project every month."

"People will just call us and tell us of a home need."

But this development could not have been possible without Radius Saluda's continual pursuit and service of the community. They were having Movie Nights on the courthouse lawn. They were grabbing their neighbors and bringing them to Super Bowl™ Parties. They were setting up Slip 'N Slide Kickball and Water Slides. They were inviting people to what they called the "Community Thanksgiving Meal"—and giving up their own Thanksgiving Day lunch to serve free Thanksgiving meals. Radius Saluda was getting hundreds (that's a *LOT* of people in Saluda) of adults and kids to attend events simply because they gave away their time, energy, and money.

That's how a church grows. That's how Radius Saluda—which began in the Harrison's barn (farm animals may or may not have walked in front of Ross as he preached), then moved to the town theatre (no, they didn't provide popcorn), then moved to Saluda High School (because every Radius plant needs a good public school to stay in), and recently bought a bank (offerings are in safe hands)—has grown to nearly one hundred and fifty people on a given Sunday. Because a few individuals decided to impact their personal radius and serve the people around them, Radius Saluda is the most ethnically and socioeconomically diverse of the Radius church plants.

Now, Trey Shealy has filled Ross Kellis's place at the helm of the church in Saluda. And this body continues to see the favor of the Lord.

Rocky Creek

In 2017, Radius in Lexington was beginning to encounter a problem: too few seats. A good problem for sure, but a problem nonetheless. It was at this time that Radius—who was already contemplating another church plant—recognized the prodding of the Lord to reproduce.

But where? When? And who would go? There were a lot of questions that needed answering if Radius was going to plant another church in Lexington. So all throughout the month of May, Radius Partners prayed and fasted once a week over the possibility of another church plant, asking God whether He wanted them (individually) to go, and where He wanted the church to go.

Then they sent out a poll to the Radius Partners. They asked if they would, in fact, be willing to go, and if they would rather a church plant toward the new high school (River Bluff), or the new elementary school (Rocky Creek). Surprisingly, the overwhelming majority asked to plant out near Rocky Creek.

....

Quick Digression: In 2016, Ryan Molony was hired as a Radius staff member.

In 2017, the Radius Elders asked Ryan to lead a new Radius Church plant.

In February of 2018, he was *leading* an entirely different church body in an entirely different location than where he began.

Talk about whiplash.

In the summer of 2017, they were still figuring out where they would be planting a church—six months later they were having services with over *120* folks who felt called (and who were heavily recruited by Ryan) to leave Lexington and impact their area.

It definitely wasn't Radius Lexington. But it wasn't supposed to be. It was supposed to be Radius Rocky Creek. "Same DNA... same bloodline... different radius."

....

As Rocky Creek first began, John Reeves was speaking at Radius Lexington's 9:15 service, and then driving over to speak at Rocky Creek's 10:15 service, and then driving back to speak at Lexington's 11:15 service. Rocky Creek was essentially *bound* to the "Mother Church."

But in no time Rocky Creek found itself growing more independent and self-sufficient. Ryan Molony increased in his role as sole leader and primary communicator, and a few families (Allred's, Krick's, Anderson's, Cogdill's, Bryan's, and several others) stepped into new roles.

Now, after a little more than two years, Rocky Creek has over three hundred people attending.

Irmo

Radius Irmo is still in its stages of infancy but has "incredible potential." This church-plant came out of the devotion of a handful of families who "have been coming to Radius and love their part of the town."

Similar to Saluda, it started with a Bible study... and then John Reeves began meeting with them. Soon enough, they found themselves meeting once a month, then every other Sunday night, and beginning on September 8th of

2019, Radius Irmo began meeting *every* week. And after handing Radius Saluda to Trey Shealy, Ross Kellis began leading the Radius Irmo church plant.

In less than a year, Irmo has grown to around a hundred attendees on a given Sunday.

....

One of the most exciting things for the people who have been at Radius for a while is to see new leaders rise up over time. "Part of how you're developed as a disciple is to carry weight," and "one of the greatest joys" of leaders at Radius is to see how the Treys and Ryans and Derricks grow into their roles of increased responsibility. Radius has always pushed to have a culture of entrusting leadership to young folks—often surprisingly quickly.

Heck, they got a *teenager* to write their book.

Part 3: "The Battle is the Lord's and We're Working"

If you've been coming to Radius in last few years, you probably know about all this stuff that's gone down recently. But if you don't go to Radius, or have only come recently, or just zone-out a lot (looking at you, Malachi Reeves), here's the lowdown:

More Building(s)

LEXINGTON: In the last few years, Radius Lexington has acquired several buildings adjacent to its main auditorium at 300 West Main Street in Lexington, South

Carolina. These buildings have provided Radius with space for Student Ministries on Sunday nights, Preschool-Elementary Children's Care on Sunday mornings, and an office for the Radius Staff. Radius Lexington has also built an atrium alongside its main building.

WHITE KNOLL: Derrick Liferidge had been praying with Pastor Dave from Chapel of Redemption for some time when the Lord "impressed upon Pastor Dave" to give Radius their facility. After many years of faithfulness, Pastor Dave and the rest of the Chapel of Redemption elected to plant a seed with their resources and "sold" their entire facility to Radius.

The cost? $5.

This facility, complete with a sanctuary, gym, and children's classrooms, was painted, landscaped, and renovated under a team of volunteers led by Joe Pitts. After Carolina Springs Elementary School generously offered up its building to lease for several years, Radius White Knoll finally received a building of their own on November 15th, 2017.

ROCKY CREEK: On March 1st of 2019, Radius received a phone call about the possibility of a building for Rocky Creek. After looking over the building, Ryan Molony, John Reeves, and Chris Seeby agreed that its location, facilities, accessibility, and price were excellent. Radius made an offer on the Diesel Laptops building... and it was accepted. After extensive renovations, Rocky Creek is looking to be in the building in early 2021, where it has been renamed to Radius *Centerville*.

<u>SALUDA</u>: Recently, Radius Saluda was able to find and buy a building right along the "[Town] Square." This building (a bank) is the newest, cleanest, and most modern of the Radius buildings (plus it has a huge safe). Radius Saluda held their first service at this location in July of 2019, and they have almost doubled in size since relocating.

<u>SOUTHSIDE</u>: Cheryl Reeves and Theresa Hodge first met as neighbors, passing by each other in their neighborhood on their walks. After a time, they became friends, and they often stopped to talk together. On one of these days, Cheryl—being the open-book, uber-extrovert that she is—started telling Theresa about all the ways God has provided Radius with buildings in the past. After Cheryl explained, Theresa looked at her and said, "That's us."

Theresa Hodge was part of a small church in Columbia, South Carolina called Southside Baptist Church which was established over a hundred years ago. As its members became fewer and older, they began considering giving up their facilities to another church...

In the following weeks and months, John Reeves spoke occasionally at Southside as Cheryl sang, introducing themselves and Radius as a whole. After much prayer and reflection, Southside Baptist Church generously, unanimously agreed to *merge* with Radius Church and offer up their facilities on June 1st, 2020 and concluded the merge in late August.

....

So there's an update on a lot of the cool opportunities Radius has had in recent years. But not everything has been so fortunate for this family of believers.

In the last two years, two of the most traumatic events in the history of Radius have taken place.

....

I don't feel that I could ever adequately write the stories of Chris McCutchan or Toby Kirkland, who each passed away well before anyone expected them to. If you want to hear their full stories, about who they were and what they did, you should speak with Wendy McCutchan or Stacey Kirkland. Even so, this book wouldn't be complete without their names. Chris McCutchan and Toby Kirkland were both pillars of Radius Church for years on end; Chris as a leader in discipleship and missional work, and Toby as an elder, mentor, and dear friend.

Both of their lives ended tragically, shockingly, leaving behind grieving families and friends. And yet, through the goodness of the Gospel, sorrow could not reign over these men and women. In fact, as I reflect on my own life, there have been a handful of moments where I have experienced God so acutely.

If I have ever seen beauty, it was in the embrace of Wendy and Jennifer McCutchan at Chris's funeral, and it was in the tear-filled laugh of Stacey Kirkland as she remembered Toby's love for her. There is one love, one hope, and one peace that can conquer death—and that only comes from Jesus Christ. Chris and Toby fought to live their lives for the God of Glory and finished well.

One day this body we have will fail, and we will see God Almighty enthroned in glory.

What will He say to you?

Long before he died, Chris wrote out his wishes for his funeral, and one wish he wrote with special emphasis: *"make sure JESUS is preached,"* Jesus in all caps. I only feel it's appropriate to share the Gospel once more now.

We are all sinners, and we all need a Savior. To save us, God the Father sent His Son, Jesus Christ, down to the earth where he was born as a human. Jesus lived a perfect life with no sin, but was crucified by the people He came to save. On that cross Jesus bore all the world's sins, and when He rose from the grave three days later, He paved the way for us to have everlasting life with God. Now, whoever *believes* in this truth and decides to follow Jesus will receive forgiveness of sins and the Holy Spirit in their heart, which is a guarantee of our new, everlasting life face-to-face with Jesus after we die.

And that's where Toby and Chris are now. Face-to-face with our Glorious King.

Part 3: "New Stuff"

New. An exciting word. It means improvement, upgrading, innovation, *change*.

New. A terrifying word. It means uncomfortable, unfamiliar, unknown, *change*.

For almost all of us, we experienced significant, *radical* change in the past year—maybe more so than in the past five or ten years combined. Radius too, in its own way, has undergone immense change. New systems, new hires, new events, new technology, new campuses... A lot of new.

And yet our God has *not* changed, and neither has our focus. We still believe God has called for us to glorify Him by making disciples, planting churches, and living generously. All our attempts at *new* reflect that conviction.

"40 Hours"

Five eight-hour days. That's how much time the Radius Elders and leaders spent together in discussion, prayer, and argument as they debated on how they would reach the maximum amount of people in Lexington and beyond with the Good News of Christ. As they continued to debate, they unanimously agreed they wanted Radius to have what they called a "***together*** voice." They wanted all the churches of Radius (Lexington, White Knoll, Saluda, Rocky Creek, Irmo) to be of one mind—to be a "Family of Churches." John Reeves would be the *Lead Pastor* of Radius as a whole, and *Campus Pastors* would lead their individual campuses.

That's when the idea of *video* came into play.

After *much* prayer (they literally set a timer to stop and pray every thirty minutes), mental and emotional exertion, and constant debate, they decided that *occasional* video (recording messages and having them displayed on a screen) was, in fact, the best way to have a united voice in the church.

Now let me tell you this before I continue: "none of the elders prefer video over live teaching." John Reeves has made fun of video for the last decade—and I've sat there listening to him. Lin Keesey, Brian Kirkland, Toby Kirkland, Chris Seeby, Tom Wood, and Clete Cordero (2019 Elder

Team) were not in favor of video at first. And neither, as you might have guessed, were some of the leaders at White Knoll, Saluda, or Rocky Creek...

"The first time I heard about it I went home and I told my wife, 'I'll have another job in two years. I don't wanna show up every Sunday and cut the TV on for somebody else.'"

Those were Ryan Molony's first words when he heard Radius was going to begin implementing video at Radius Church (totally just threw him under the bus, but it's all for a good cause). Yet over time, "the Lord has worked on [Ryan's] heart," and Ryan explained to Radius Church at its Partner Meeting in August of 2019, "It's not about me."

It's not about John Reeves on that screen. It wasn't about Todd Carnes on that stage. It's not about you or me. It's about Christ. And Radius decided that it will best exalt Christ in their area by working *together* as one church meeting with multiple congregations.

Lexington, White Knoll, Saluda, Rocky Creek, Irmo, Southside, and any other church plant in the future, each glorifying God in its own unique way but sharing resources and vision.

As a result of this new process which required extensive organization, Radius finally came to the conclusion that they were in need of an Executive Pastor, someone who might help keep the unorganized tendencies of Radius in check.

I know what you're thinking: *who would be crazy enough to take that job?*

Well, after months of interviews, the elders finally found some guy named Jerry Dominic (if you've snoozed through this book, I may need to remind you of Jerry's huge involvement with Todd Carnes) and he and Alison moved back to Lexington from Florida after several years break. And for the first time in, well, *ever*, Radius—who would have thought this day would come—is embarking on a journey from "organized chaos" to "somewhat organized."

COVID-19

Talk about new—*everything* changed for everyone once COVID hit. Hectic doesn't begin to express the difficulties of decision-making. And wise choices were crucial. People were hurting, struggling under both the nature of the virus and the suffering economy.

So we gave them chicken—and suntans.

GROCERIES ON THE GO:

There was a line all the way out of the back of the Radius (Lexington) parking lot. A refrigerated semi-truck full of Amick Farms chicken was parked alongside the front of the Radius building. Across from the semi was another truck, chock-full of Senn Brothers produce. For hours on end, cars would drive in between those two trucks as Radius high school and college students would load boxes of produce, wings, or tenders in the trunks of cars.

Thousands of pounds of produce and chicken were gone by the day's end.

As COVID ramped up and employment rates went down, Radius Church partnered with Amick Farms (chicken) and Senn Brothers (produce) to provide cheap food (which was pre-ordered online), and to raise money for people in need. After executing "Groceries-On-The-Go" multiple times, Radius was able to give away all their proceeds: $40,000 to hairdressers and waitresses in the area, and $15,000 to Ezekiel Ministries and Mission Lexington.

THE CHURCH IS NOT A BUILDING:

Funny thing: because Radius had made the tough decision to run video in 2019, they already had the equipment to go online when COVID-19 broke out. Radius spent nine weeks with online teaching as John Reeves and campus pastors Russell Johnson, Derrick Liferidge, Ryan Molony, Ross Kellis, and Trey Shealy (throwback to when Trey left his fly open on camera) led Radius through a very difficult season, which included Good Friday and Easter Sunday. By week nine, though, the leadership of Radius made a new decision: on May 17 they would meet in person once more...

Sunburns and Showmobiles

After over a decade serving on staff at Radius *and* as an elder; after leading many of Radius' innovative efforts since the beginning; after *thousands* of Chick-fil-A meetings and a wide variety of humorous, somewhat "edgy" Sunday morning announcements; after overseeing and leading Radius through the best and worst of times, Chris Seeby decided it was time for him to step out of his work at the helm of Radius and begin something new in early 2020.

When the Coronavirus hit, it seemed like the perfect time for Chris and Cortney Seeby to quietly faze out as vast changes washed over Radius. They would still attend and serve at Radius Lexington, but this would be their first break from the weight of Radius responsibility in over *fifteen years*. Their drive, presence, and leadership was part of the glue that held Radius together in the most difficult times. In the words of a multiple Radius leaders: "they represented exactly who we [Radius] wanted to be."

Enter the Johnson family.

In 2018, Russell and Teri Johnson moved their five kids from Texas to join Radius, where Russell served as Teaching Pastor. In May of 2020, Russell was officially named the Campus Pastor of Radius Lexington as Chris Seeby exited his work at Radius. And on his first Sunday as Campus Pastor, he stood on the "Showmobile" (a portable semi-truck trailer that unfolds into a stage), looking into the sun, which, for all the talk about rain, was shining as brightly as ever, heating up the asphalt parking lot where people sat in lawn chairs outside Radius's building.

Ninety-degree weather was not exactly what he had in mind for their first time regathering.

In fact, three services later, Russell was sweating through his shirt, he had a slight burn on his bald head, and his voice was hoarse from trying to speak over the cars, sirens, and frolicking children.

And yet, that morning Radius was able to reach people it had never reached before. People driving on Main Street would hear the band and pull in to check it out; dog-walkers and morning-joggers would take detours and hang out in the back of the parking lot to listen.

Obviously, Radius didn't match their attendance numbers pre-COVID. Even so, there's something about the way the church continues to gather even in the face of oppression, even in the face of danger, even in the face of discomfort. This doesn't mean we gather recklessly—air hugs, elbow bumps, extra sanitizer, and distanced seating were mandated—but we gather purposefully, to rejoice in each other, and to proclaim the death of Christ until He returns.

So Russell endured a little sweat... and we all got a nice tan.

....

RADIUS Lexington met in their parking lot.

RADIUS White Knoll met in their parking lot, and then got themselves a showmobile too.

RADIUS Rocky Creek met outside their new building in the grass (also showmobile-style).

RADIUS Saluda met on the Saluda Courthouse Lawn, then in Saluda Park.

And RADIUS Irmo met under a very large tree.

The church is not a building, and it's not a streaming service either. The church is the people who follow Christ, and we love to be in community.

MVP

Random shout-out #1 to Andy Ott and the tech team for doing all the stuff they did that makes sense to nobody else over COVID. Without them, online services/outdoor services would have been a nightmare. Andy definitely takes home the MVP for the COVID season.

Random shout-out #2 to Brian Kirkland and Andrea Krick for the idea and execution of the Radius lawn chairs.

Radius created a BYOChair policy for safe outdoor services, and Brian Kirkland came up with the idea of giving out free lawn chairs to all Radius Partners. Andrea handled the rest. She tends to handle a lot of the random, spur-of-the-moment Radius things... always behind-the-scenes.

Southside (Downtown Columbia)

You may remember that seventeen years ago "Radius" was actually born in Downtown Columbia before it merged with "Oasis" and transitioned to Lexington, South Carolina. You might recall that a group of the leaders were crushed that Radius would focus its efforts away from the city of Columbia.

Now, after these seventeen years, Radius has grown and branched into five campuses within the Midlands area—and we are looking to move further...

Into Downtown Columbia.

....

Scott Shuford was living in Traveler's Rest with his wife Jess and their four boys. Six acres. A pond. A creek. A great church and community. Who could ask for more?

And yet Scott was "unsettled."

It was November of 2019, and Scott had just talked with John Reeves (whom he had met at Radius Greenville, helping to plant that church). John had thrown out the idea of Scott moving to Columbia, SC (basically the exact opposite of picturesque Traveler's Rest—probably because it's Gamecock territory) to plant a church—and Scott was actually thinking about it.

"Stop thinking like that!" He wanted to tell himself. *"Why would I ever want to risk this?"*

As a mother of four in an excellent environment, Jess was even more skeptical. And Scott began pursuing another job.

In December, though, Scott and Jess decided to spend the day with John and Cheryl Reeves, Joe and Meg Pitts, Derrick and Tessa Liferidge, and several other Radius staff members and families. They talked, prayed, and discussed possibilities, scoped out downtown, and then went home. Scott and Jess loved it. But they drove in silence all the way back to Traveler's Rest.

Then, on January 1st, both of Scott's opportunities were slammed to an abrupt close.

When reflecting on his and Jess's next decision, Scott told me this, "I've never prayed and fasted [for guidance] about something more, and I've never been more sure of anything."

After much thought, Jess came to Scott one day and told him she was willing to move from their little paradise and head to Columbia—which isn't exactly known for its family-fun environment (again, Gamecock territory...).

And even when the "Coronavirus" hit just as they put their house on the market, even though their six acres and pond and creek were picture-perfect, even though no one knew what was about to happen with church-planting (virtual church? socially-distanced church?), the Shuford's have moved to Columbia, and have begun their new journey as church-planters.

Columbia. Irmo. Centerville (Rocky Creek). Saluda. White Knoll. Lexington.

Will you go too?

Todd Carnes stepped out of his role leading Radius as John Reeves stepped in. Meanwhile, Radius has planted churches in Saluda, Gilbert, Irmo, and Columbia. After drastic changes (and unique services) caused by COVID, Radius is slowly working on returning to a state of normalcy, pushing forward to navigate new challenges in ministry.

To Be Continued

So now you know. You know how Radius Church began with six adults and six kids. You know how this body has grown in backyards, apartments, public schools, coffeeshops, theatres, banks, Ace Hardwares, and Diesel Laptops buildings. You know how the men and women of early Radius gave up what the world tells us are "successful lives" of pleasure, comfort, and luxury to follow their Lord Jesus Christ. You know how they did stupid things, how they did crazy things, how they wept, how they prayed, how they sang, how they dreamed…

And you know how the LORD of Hosts has answered them time and time again. You know how God provided them with every good thing. You know how the LORD moved in these families—telling them to go or stay. You know how *He* gave them their leaders, their buildings, their favor with their communities. *He* changed hearts. *He* transformed lives.

Hopefully you know that He is real. That despite the year we had in 2020, our God has not stopped moving, and He will continue moving in 2021 just as He was moving in 2003.

What you don't know—and what I don't know—is how many pages this book will have a few years from now…

So my question for you is, *will you be a part of it?* Will you hand out roses, or open up your home, or buy someone else's building, or move your whole family because you are chasing after God? Will you go to pray at 5am, or walk away from a lucrative career, or leave an established campus to start up a smaller one simply because you value God's desires more than your own? Will you risk unemployment, or give away your car, or take a pay-cut, or dedicate the best hours of your day to impact your radius?

Maybe you're new to Christianity or generosity or RADIUS and these all seem like terribly difficult steps to take. It might be that the Chris Seebys and Brian Kirklands and Cheryl Reeves and Laurie Keeseys of the world are a little intimidating to imitate. In truth, these are just real people with real faith in Jesus.

But let's start small anyway, and we can work out from there.

Do you know your neighbor's name?

Summer, 2003. First meeting of Radius Church.

Made in the USA
Middletown, DE
18 February 2022

61330098R00068